Who Should Read This Book?

We've all heard the scenario: the family on vacation stops at a road-side "dig your own" gem mine. Junior finds a sapphire the size of a peach and ends up on national television telling the world how he will spend his fortune.

T This book is for those who have read these stories and want their chance to find their own fortune. It is also a book for those who would enjoy the adventure of finding a few gems, getting them cut or polished, and making their own jewelry. It is a book for those people who want to plan a gem hunting vacation with their family. It is a book for those who study the metaphysical properties of gems and minerals and would like to add to their personal collections.

T This book is for those who would like to keep the art of rock-hounding alive and pass it on to their children. It is a book on where to find your own gems and minerals and on how to begin what for many is a lifelong hobby.

T This is a book for those who aren't interested in the "hidden treasure map through mosquito-infested no-man's-land" approach to treasure hunting but do want to find gems and minerals. It is for those who want to get out the pick and shovel and get a little dirty. (Although at some mines they bring the buckets of pre-dug dirt to you at an environmentally temper-ature controlled sluicing area.)

Many an unsuspecting tourist has stopped at a mine to try his or her luck and become a rockhound for life. Watch out! Your collection may end up taking the place of your car in your garage.

Good hunting!

This volume is one in a four-volume series.

VOLUME 4

VOLUME 3

VOLUME 1

VOLUME 2

The Treasure Hunter's

GEM & MINERAL
GUIDES TO THE U.S.A.

2ND EDITION

Where & How to Dig, Pan, and Mine Your Own Gems & Minerals

VOLUME 1: NORTHWEST STATES

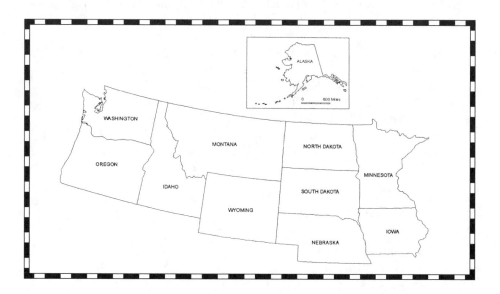

by KATHY J. RYGLE AND STEPHEN F. PEDERSEN
Preface by Antoinette Matlins, P.G.,
author of *Gem Identification Made Easy*

GemStone Press
Woodstock, Vermont

The Treasure Hunter's Gem & Mineral Guides to the U.S.A.: 2nd Edition
Where & How to Dig, Pan, and Mine Your Own Gems & Minerals
Volume 1: Northwest States

2003 Second Edition
© 2003 by Kathy J. Rygle and Stephen F. Pedersen
Preface © 2003 by Antoinette Matlins

1999 First Edition

Library of Congress Cataloging-in-Publication Data
Rygle, Kathy J., 1955–
    Northwest treasure hunter's gem & mineral guide : where & how to dig, pan, and mine your own gems & minerals / Kathy J. Rygle and Stephen F. Pedersen—2nd ed.
        p.   cm.
    Rev. ed. of: The treasure hunter's gem & mineral guides to the U.S.A. c1999.
    Includes index.
    ISBN 0-943763-37-1 (NW)—ISBN 0-943763-40-1 (SE)—
ISBN 0-943763-38-X (SW)—ISBN 0-943763-39-8 (NE)
    1. Minerals—Collection and preservation—United States—Guidebooks.
    2. Precious stones—Collection and preservation—United States—Guidebooks.
    3. United States—Guidebooks. I. Pedersen, Stephen F., 1948– II. Rygle, Kathy J., 1955– Treasure hunter's gem & mineral guides to the U.S.A. III. Title.

    QE375.R92 2003
    549.973—dc21

2003040801

Cover design: Bronwen Battaglia
Text design: Chelsea Dippel

10 9 8 7 6 5 4 3 2 1

Manufactured in the United States of America

Published by GemStone Press
A Division of LongHill Partners, Inc.
Sunset Farm Offices, Route 4, P.O. Box 237
Woodstock, VT 05091
Tel: (802) 457-4000   Fax: (802) 457-4004
www.gemstonepress.com

Dedications, with love, to our parents and children:

To my parents, Joe and Helen Rygle, who taught me the love of nature; my earliest remembrances of "rockhounding" are hikes with my dad in the fields, forests, and streams near our home. I also remember weekend trips with my mother to a shop that sold specimens of minerals from around the world. To my daughter, Annie Rygle, who shares with me and continues to show me the wonders of nature. Also, thanks to Annie for helping me sort the information for the updates. —K. J. R.

To my parents, Cliff and Leone Pedersen, who taught me to value nature and to not quit. To my daughters Kristi and Debbie, who challenge me to keep growing. —S. F. P.

To our combined families, including Georgia Pedersen, and to family no longer with us.

With special thanks:

To all the owners of fee dig mines and guide services, curators and staff of public and private museums, mine owners, and miners. Our thanks to all those individuals both past and present who share the wonders of the earth with us.

To our agent, Barb Doyen, and her childhood rock collection.

To our publisher, Stuart M. Matlins, editor Emily Wichland, and all the staff at GemStone Press for their guidance, assistance, and patience.

To Mrs. Betty Jackson for, in her own way, telling Kathy to write the book.

To God and the wonders He has given us.

And finally, to each other, with love and the perseverance to keep on trying.

Volume 1—Northwest States

CONTENTS

PREFACE

All-American Gems

by Antoinette Matlins, P.G.

When Americans think of costly and fabled gems, they associate them with exotic origins—Asia, South Africa or Brazil. They envision violent jungle quests or secret cellars of a sultanate, perhaps scenes from a Jorge Amado novel or from *A Thousand and One Nights*, a voluptuous Indian princess whose sari is adorned with the plentiful rubies and sapphires of her land, or a Chinese emperor sitting atop a throne flanked by dragons carved from exquisitely polished jade.

Asked what gems are mined in the United States, most Americans would probably draw a blank. We know our country is paved with one of the finest highway systems in the world, but we don't know that just below the surface, and sometimes on top of it, is a glittering pavement of gemstones that would color Old Glory. The red rubies of North Carolina, the white diamonds of Arkansas, the blue sapphires of Montana—America teems with treasures that its citizens imagine come from foreign lands. These include turquoise, tourmaline, amethyst, pearls, opals, jade, sapphires, emeralds, rubies, and even gem-quality diamonds.

Not only does America have quantity, it has quality. American gems compare very favorably with gems from other countries. In fact, fine gemstones found in the U.S. can rival specimens from anywhere else in the world. Some gems, like the luxurious emerald-green hiddenite and steely blue benitoite, are found only in America. Others, like the tourmalines of Maine and California, rival specimens found in better-known locations such as Brazil and Zambia.

The discovery of gemstones in U.S. terrain has been called a lost chapter in American history. It continues to be a saga of fashion and fable that, like the stones themselves, are a deep part of our national heritage. Appreciation of our land's generous yield of sparkling colored stones reached a zenith at the end of the nineteenth century with the art nouveau movement and its utilization of them. When the Boer Wars ended, South Africa's diamonds and platinum eclipsed many of our own then so-called semiprecious stones. Not until the 1930s, and again starting with the 1960s, did economics and the yen for color make gems more desirable again.

In the late 1800s, the nation sought out and cherished anything that was unique to the land. The search for gemstones in America coincided with the exploration of the West, and nineteenth-century mineralogists, some bonafide and others self-proclaimed, fulfilled that first call for "Made in America." Their discoveries created sensations not only throughout America but in the capitals of Europe and as far away as China. The Europeans, in fact, caught on before the Americans, exhibiting some of America's finest specimens in many of Europe's great halls.

But the search for gemstones in this country goes back even further than the nineteenth century. In 1541, the Spanish explorer Francisco Coronado trekked north from Mexico in the footsteps of Cortés and Pizarro, searching not only for gold but also for turquoise, amethyst and emeralds. In the early 1600s, when English settlers reached Virginia, they had been instructed "to searche for gold and such jewels as ye may find."

But what eluded the Spanish explorers and early settlers was unearthed by their descendants. Benitoite, which may be our nation's most uniquely attractive gem, was discovered in 1907 in California's San Benito River headwaters. A beautiful, rare gem with the color of fine sapphire and the fire of a diamond, benitoite is currently found in gem quality only in San Benito, California.

Like many of America's finest stones discovered during the "Gem Rush" of the nineteenth century, benitoite was held in higher regard throughout the rest of the world than it was on its native U.S. soil.

The gem occurs most commonly in various shades of blue. A fine-quality blue benitoite can resemble fine blue sapphire, but it is even more brilliant. It has one weakness, however: in comparison to sapphire, it is relatively soft. It is therefore best used in pendants, brooches and earrings, or in rings with a protective setting.

While benitoite is among the rarest of our gems, our riches hardly stop there. America is the source of other unusual gems, including three even more uniquely American stones, each named after an American: kunzite, hiddenite and morganite.

The story of all-American kunzite is inseparable from the achievements of two men: Charles Lewis Tiffany, founder of Tiffany & Co., and Dr. George Frederick Kunz, world-renowned gemologist. By seeking, collecting and promoting gems found in America, these two did more for the development of native stones than anyone else during, or since, their time.

While working for Tiffany in the late 1800s, Dr. Kunz received a package in the mail containing a stone that the sender believed to be an unusual tourmaline. The stone came from an abandoned mine at Pala Mountain, California, where collectors had found traces of spodumene—a gemstone prized by the ancients but which no one had been able to find for many years. Dr. Kunz was ecstatic to find before him a specimen of "extinct spodumene of a gloriously lilac color." A fellow gemologist, Dr. Charles Baskerville, named the find "kunzite" in his honor.

Kunzite has become a favorite of such designers as Paloma Picasso, not only because of its distinctive shades—lilac, pink, and yellow-green orchid—but because it is one of a diminishing number of gems available in very large sizes at affordable prices. It is a perfect choice for the centerpiece around which to create a very bold, dramatic piece of jewelry. Designer Picasso's creations include a magnificent necklace using a 400-carat kunzite. Although it is a moderately hard stone, kunzite is easily fractured, and care must be taken to avoid any sharp blows.

Kunzite's sister gem, hiddenite, is also a truly "all-American" stone. In 1879, William Earl Hidden, an engraver and mineralogist, was sent to North Carolina on behalf of the great American inventor and prospector Thomas Alva Edison to search for platinum. Hidden found none of the precious white metal but in his pursuit unearthed a new green gemstone, which was named "hiddenite" in his honor.

Less well known than kunzite, hiddenite is an exquisite, brilliant emerald-green variety of spodumene not found anyplace else in the world. While light green and yellow-green shades have been called hiddenite, the Gemological Institute of America—this country's leading authority on gemstones—considers only the emerald-green shade of spodumene, found exclusively in the Blue Ridge Mountains of Mitchell County, North Carolina, to be true hiddenite.

The foothills of the Blue Ridge Mountains also possess America's most significant emerald deposits. While output is minimal compared to Colombia, Zambia or Pakistan, the Rist Mine in Hiddenite, North Carolina, has produced some very fine emeralds, comparable to Colombian stones. The discovery was first made by a farmer plowing his field who found them lying loose on the soil. The country folk, not knowing what they had come across, called the stones "green bolts."

In August 1970, a 26-year-old "rock hound" named Wayne Anthony found a glowing 59-carat "green bolt" at the Rist Mine only two feet from the surface. It was cut into a 13.14-carat emerald of very fine color. Tiffany & Co. later purchased the stone and called it the Carolina Emerald. "The gem is superb," said Paul E. Desautels, then the curator of mineralogy at the Smithsonian Institution. "It can stand on its own merits as a fine and lovely gem of emerald from anywhere, including Colombia." In 1973, the emerald became the official state stone of North Carolina.

A California prize, the warm peach- or pink-shaded morganite, was named by Dr. Kunz for financier John Pierpont Morgan, who purchased the Bement gem collection for donation to the American Museum of Natural History in New York, where it can be viewed today. Morganite is a member of the beryl family, which gives us aquamarine (the clear blue variety of beryl) and emerald (the deep green variety of beryl). However, morganite is available in much larger sizes than its mineralogical cousins and is much more affordable.

Many consider the core of our national treasure chest to be gems like the tourmalines of Maine and California and the sapphires of Montana, gems that are mined in commercial quantities and have earned worldwide reputations. One day in the fall of 1820, two young boys, Ezekiel Holmes and Elijah Hamlin, were rock hunting on Mount Mica in Oxford County, Maine. On the way home, one of the boys saw a flash of green light coming from underneath an uprooted tree. The find was later identified as tourmaline, and Mount Mica became the site of the first commercial gem mine in the United States. The mine was initially worked by Elijah Hamlin and his brother Hannibal, who later became Abraham Lincoln's vice president.

The colors of the rainbow meld delicately in the tourmalines of Maine, producing some of the finest specimens in the world, rivaling in quality even those from Brazil. A 150-mile strip in central Maine provides shades of apple green, burgundy red and salmon pink, to mention just a few. Some stones are bi-colored.

Miners are kept busy in the Pala district of San Diego County, California, as well. California, in fact, is North America's largest producer of gem-quality tourmaline.

The hot-pink tourmalines, for which California is famous, began to come into greater demand in 1985, as pastel-colored stones became more and more coveted by chic women around the globe. Curiously enough, over one hundred years ago the Chinese rejoiced in the fabulous colors of this fashionable stone. The Empress Dowager of the Last Chinese Imperial Dynasty sent emissaries to California in search of pink tourmalines. She garnished her robes with carved tourmaline buttons and toggles, and started a fad which overtook China. Much of the empress's collection of fine carvings was lost or stolen when the dynasty fell around 1912, but artifacts made from California's pink tourmaline can be seen today in a Beijing museum. China's fascination with pink tourmalines lasted long after the empress. In 1985, a contingent of the Chinese Geological Survey came to California with two requests: to see Disneyland and the Himalaya Mine, original site of California pink tourmaline.

While the Chinese are mesmerized by our tourmalines, Americans have always been attracted to China's jade. But perhaps we ought to take stock of our own. Wyoming, in fact, is the most important producer of the stone in the Western Hemisphere. The state produces large quantities of good-quality green nephrite jade—the type most commonly used in jewelry and carvings. California also boasts some jade, as does Alaska. Chinese immigrants panning for gold in California in the late 1800s found large boulders of nephrite and sent them back to China, where the jade was carved and sold within China and around the world.

The U.S. is also one of the largest producers of turquoise. Americans mostly associate this stone with American Indian jewelry, but its use by mainstream designers has regularly come in and out of fashion.

Some of the most prized gems of America are the stunning sapphires from Yogo Gulch, Montana. These sapphires emit a particularly pleasing shade of pale blue, and are known for their clarity and brilliance.

The Montana mine was originally owned by a gold-mining partnership. In 1895, an entire summer's work netted a total of only $700 in gold plus a cigar box full of heavy blue stones. The stones were sent to Tiffany & Co. to be identified. Tiffany then sent back a check for $3,750 for the entire box of obviously valuable stones.

Once one can conceive of gem-quality sapphires in America, it takes only a small stretch of the mind to picture the wonderful diamonds found here. A 40.23-carat white gem found in Murfreesboro, Arkansas, was cut into a 14.42-carat emerald-cut diamond named Uncle Sam. Other large diamonds include a 23.75-carat diamond found in the mid-nineteenth century in Manchester, Virginia, and a greenish 34.46-carat diamond named the Punch Jones, which was claimed to have been found in Peterstown, West Virginia.

Each year, thousands of people visit Crater of Diamonds State Park in Arkansas, where, for a fee, they can mine America's only proven location of gem-quality diamonds. Among them is a group known as "regulars" who visit the park looking for their "retirement stone."

In 1983, one of the regulars, 82-year-old Raymond Shaw, came across a 6.7-carat rough diamond. He sold it for $15,000 uncut. According to Mark Myers, assistant superintendent of the state park, the stone was cut into an exceptionally fine, 2.88-carat gem (graded E/Flawless by the Gemological Institute of America). Myers says the cut stone, later called the Shaw Diamond, was offered for sale for $58,000.

Diamonds have also been found along the shores of the Great Lakes, in many localities in California, in the Appalachian Mountains, in Illinois, Indiana, Ohio, Kentucky, New York, Idaho and Texas. Exploration for diamonds continues in Michigan, Wisconsin, Colorado and Wyoming, according to the U.S. Bureau of Mines. The discovery of gem-quality diamonds in Alaska in 1986 initiated a comprehensive search there for man's most valued gem.

Many questions concerning this country's store of gems remain unanswered. "Numerous domestic deposits of semiprecious gem stones are known and have been mined for many years," wrote the Bureau of Mines in a 1985 report. "However, no systematic evaluations of the magnitude of these deposits have been made and no positive statements can be made about them." Even as the United States continues to offer up its kaleidoscopic range of gems, our American soil may hold a still greater variety and quantity of gems yet to be unearthed.

And here, with the help of these down-to-earth (in the best possible way!)

guides, you can experience America's gem and mineral riches for yourself. In these pages rockhounds, gemologists, vacationers, and families alike will find a hands-on introduction to the fascinating world of gems and minerals . . . and a treasure map to a sparkling side of America. Happy digging!

T

Antoinette Matlins, P.G. is an internationally respected gem and jewelry expert, author and lecturer. Active in the gem trade and a popular media guest, she has been seen on ABC, CBS, NBC, and CNN, educating consumers about gems and jewelry and exposing fraud. Her books include *Jewelry & Gems: The Buying Guide; Jewelry & Gems at Auction: The Definitive Guide to Buying & Selling at the Auction House & on Internet Auction Sites; Engagement & Wedding Rings: The Definitive Buying Guide for People in Love; The Pearl Book: The Definitive Buying Guide;* and *Gem Identification Made Easy: A Hands-On Guide to More Confident Buying & Selling* (all GemStone Press).

Introduction

This is a guide to commercially operated gem and mineral mines (fee dig mines) within the United States that offer would-be treasure hunters the chance to "dig their own," from diamonds to thundereggs.

For simplicity, the term *fee dig site* is used to represent all types of fee-based mines or collection sites. However, for liability reasons, many mines no longer let collectors dig their own dirt, but rather dig it for them and provide it in buckets or bags. Some fee-based sites involve surface collection.

This book got its start when the authors, both environmental scientists, decided to make their own wedding rings. Having heard stories about digging your own gems, they decided to dig their own stones for their rings. So off to Idaho and Montana they went, taking their three children, ages 8, 13, and 15 at the time, in search of opals and garnets, their birthstones. They got a little vague information before and during the trip on where to find gem mines and in the process got lost in some of those "mosquito-infested lands." But when they did find actual "dig your own" mines (the kind outlined in this book), they found opals, garnets, and even sapphires. They have since made other trips to fee dig mines and each time have come home with treasures and some incredible memories.

The authors are also now the proud owners of a set of lapidary equipment, i.e., rock saw and rock polisher. They first used them to cut thundereggs collected from a mine in Oregon. The next project was to trim the many pounds of fossil fish rocks they acquired at a fee dig fossil site. The sequel to this guide series will cover authorized fossil collecting sites as well as museums on fossils and dinosaurs. It will include such topics as where to view and even make plaster casts of actual dinosaur tracks. There are even museums where kids of all ages can dig up a full-sized model of a dinosaur!

Types of Sites

The purpose of this book is principally to guide the reader to fee dig mine sites. These are gem or mineral mines where you hunt for the gem or mineral in ore at or from the mine. At fee dig sites where you are actually permitted to go into the field and dig for yourself, you will normally be shown what the gem or mineral you are seeking looks like in its natural state (much different from the polished or cut stone). Often someone is available to go out in the field with you and show you where to dig. At sites where you purchase gem- or mineral-bearing ore (either native or enriched) for washing in a flume, the process is the same: there will usually be examples of rough stones for comparison, and help in identifying your finds.

Also included are a few areas that are not fee dig sites but that are well-defined collecting sites, usually parks or beaches.

Guided field trips are a little different. Here the guide may or may not have examples of what you are looking for, but he or she will be with you in the field to help in identifying finds.

For the more experienced collector, there are field collecting areas where you are on your own in identifying what you have found. Several fee areas and guided field trips appropriate for the experienced collector are available. Check out the listings for Ruggles Mine (Grafton, NH); Harding Mine (Dixon, NM); Poland Mining Camps (Poland, ME); Perhams (West Paris, ME); and Gem Mountain Quarry Trips (Spruce Pine, NC).

Knowing What You're Looking For

Before you go out into the field, it is a good idea to know what you are looking for. Most of the fee dig mines listed in this guide will show you specimens before you set out to find your own. If you are using a guide service, you have the added bonus of having a knowledgeable person with you while you search to help you find the best place to look and help you identify your finds.

Included here is a listing of museums that contain rock and gem exhibits. A visit to these museums will help prepare you for your search. You may find examples of gems in the rough and examples of mineral specimens similar to the ones you will be looking for. Museums will most likely have displays of gems or minerals native to the local area. Some of the gems and minerals listed in this guide are of significant interest, and specimens of them can be found in museums around the country. Displays accompanying the exhibits might tell you how the gems and minerals were found, and their place in our nation's history. Many museums also hold collecting field trips or geology programs, or may be able to put you in touch with local rock and lapidary clubs.

For more information on learning how to identify your finds yourself—and even how to put together a basic portable "lab" to use at the sites—the book *Gem Identification Made Easy* by Antoinette Matlins and A. C. Bonanno (GemStone Press) is a good resource.

Rock shops are another excellent place to view gem and mineral specimens before going out to dig your own. A listing of rock shops would be too extensive to include in a book such as this. A good place to get information on rock shops in the area you plan to visit is to contact the chamber of commerce for that area. Rock shops may be able to provide information not only on rockhounding field trips but also on local rock clubs that sponsor trips.

Through mine tours you can see how minerals and gems were and are taken from the earth. On these tours, visitors learn what miners go through to remove the ores from the earth. This will give you a better appreciation for those sparkly gems you see in the showroom windows, and for many of the items we all take for granted in daily use.

You will meet other rockhounds at the mine. Attending one of the yearly events listed in the guide will also give you the chance to meet people who share your interest in gems and minerals and exchange ideas, stories, and knowledge of the hobby.

How to Use This Guide

To use this book, you can pick a state and determine what mining is available there, or pick a gem or mineral and determine where to go to "mine" it.

In this guide are indexes that will make the guide simple to use. If you are interested in finding a particular gem or mineral, go to the Index by Gem or Mineral in the back of the book. In this index, gems and minerals are listed in alphabetical order with the states and cities where fee dig sites for that gem or mineral may be found.

If you are interested in learning of sites near where you live, or in the area where you are planning a vacation, or if you simply want to know whether there are gems and minerals in a particular location, go to the Index by State, located in the back of the guide. The state index entries are broken down into three categories: Fee Dig Sites/Guide Services, Museums and Mine Tours, and Special Events and Tourist Information.

There are also several special indexes for use in finding your birthstone, anniversary stone, or zodiac stone.

Site Listings

The first section of each chapter lists fee dig sites and guide services that are available in each state. Included with the location of each site is a description of the site, directions to find it, what equipment is provided, and what you must supply. Costs are listed, along with specific policies of the site. Also included are other services available at the site and information on camping, lodging, etc. in the area of the site. Included in the section with fee dig sites are guide services for collecting gems and minerals.

In the second section of each chapter, museums of special interest to the gem/mineral collector and mine tours available to the public are listed. Besides being wonderful ways to learn about earth science, geology, and mining history (many museums and tours also offer child-friendly exhibits), museums are particularly useful for viewing gems and minerals in their rough or natural state before going out in the field to search for them.

The third section of each chapter lists special events involving gems and minerals, and resources for general tourist information.

A sample of the listings for fee dig mines and guide services (Section 1 in the guides) is on the next page.

Tips for mining:

1. Learn what gems or minerals can be found at the mine you are going to visit.

2. Know what the gem or mineral that you're hunting looks like in the rough before you begin mining.

Visiting local rock shops and museums will help in this effort.

3. When in doubt, save any stone that you are unsure about. Have an expert at the mine or at a local rock shop help you identify your find.

Sample Fee Dig Site Listing

TOWN in which the site is located / *Native or enriched[1]* • *Easy, moderate, difficult[2]*

Dig your own T

The following gems may be found:
• List of gems and minerals found at the mine

Mine name
Owner or contact (where available)
Address
Phone number
Fax
E-mail address
Website address

Open: Months, hours, days
Info: Descriptive text regarding the site, including whether equipment is provided

Admission: Fee to dig; costs for predug dirt

Other services available
Other area attractions (at times)
Information on lodging or campground facilities (where available)
Directions

Map (where available)

Notes:

1. Native or enriched. *Native* refers to gems or minerals found in the ground at the site, put there by nature. *Enriched* means that gems and minerals from an outside source have been brought in and added to the soil. Enriching is also called "salting"—it is a guaranteed return. Whatever is added in a salted mine is generally the product of some commercial mine elsewhere. Thus, it is an opportunity to "find" gemstones from around the world the easy way, instead of traveling to jungles and climbing mountains in remote areas of the globe. Salted mines are particularly nice for giving children the opportunity to find a wide variety of gems and become involved in gem identification. The authors have tried to indicate if a mine is enriched, but to be sure, ask at the mine beforehand. If the status could not be determined, this designation was left out.

2. Sites are designated as easy, moderate, or difficult. This was done to give you a feel for what a site may be like. You should contact the site and make a determination for yourself if you have any doubts.

Easy: This might be a site where the gem hunter simply purchases bags or buckets of predug dirt, washes the ore in a flume or screens the gem-bearing gravel to concentrate the gems, and flips the screen. The gems or minerals are then picked out of the material remaining in the screen. A mine which has set aside a pile of mine material for people to pick through would be another type of site designated as "Easy."

Moderate: Mining at a "Moderate" site might mean digging with a shovel, then loading the dirt into buckets, followed by sifting and sluicing. Depending on your knowledge of mineral identification, work at a "Moderate" site might include searching the surface of the ground at an unsupervised area for a gem or mineral you are not familiar with (this could also be considered difficult).

Difficult: This might be a site requiring tools such as picks and shovels, or sledgehammers and chisels. The site may be out of the way and/or difficult to get to. Mining might involve heavy digging with the pick and shovel or breaking gems or minerals out of base rock using a sledge or chisel.

Special Note:

Although most museums and many fee dig sites are handicapped accessible, please check with the listing directly.

Maps

Maps are included to help you locate the sites in the guide. At the beginning of each state, there is a state map showing the general location of towns where sites are located.

Local maps are included in a listing when the information was available. *These maps are not drawn to scale!* These maps provide information to help you get to the site but are not intended to be a substitute for a road map. Please check directly with the site you are interested in for more detailed directions.

Fees

Fees listed in these guides were obtained when the book was updated, and may have changed. They are included to give you at least a general idea of the costs you will be dealing with. Please contact the site directly to confirm charges.

Many museums have discounts for members and for groups, as well as special programs for school groups. Please check directly with the institution for information. Many smaller and/or private institutions have no fee, but do appreciate donations to help meet the costs of staying open.

Many sites accept credit cards; some may not. Please check ahead for payment options if this is important.

Requesting Information by Mail

When requesting information by mail, it is always appreciated if you send a SASE (self-addressed stamped envelope) along with your request. Doing this will often speed up the return of information.

Equipment and Safety Precautions

Equipment

The individual sites listed in these guides often provide equipment at the mine. Please note that some fee dig sites place limitations on the equipment you can use at their site. Those limitations will be noted where the information was available. Always abide by the limitations; remember that you are a guest at the site.

On the following pages are figures showing equipment for rockhounding. Figures A and B identify some of the equipment you may be told you need at a site. Figure C shows material needed to collect, package, transport, and record your findings. Figure D illustrates typical safety equipment.

Always use safety glasses with side shields or goggles when you are hammering or chiseling. Chips of rock or metal from your tools can fly off at great speed in any direction when hammering. Use gloves to protect your hands as well.

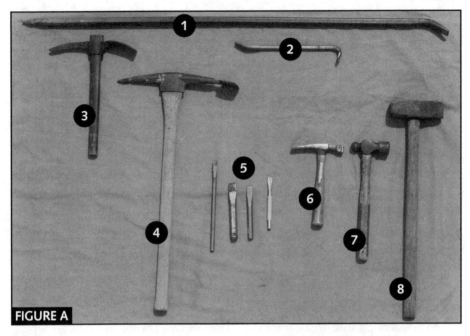

FIGURE A

1. Crowbar
2. Pry bar
3. Smaller pick
4. Rock pick
5. Various-sized chisels (*Note:* When working with a hammer and chisel, you may want to use a chisel holder, not shown, for protecting your hand if you miss. Always use eye protection with side shields and gloves!)
6. Rock hammer (*Note:* Always use eye protection.)
7. 3-pound hammer (*Note:* Always use eye protection.)
8. Sledgehammer (*Note:* When working with a sledgehammer, wear hard-toed boots along with eye protection.)

Other useful tools not shown include an ultraviolet hand lamp, and a hand magnifier.

Not pictured, but something you don't want to forget, is your camera and plenty of extra film. You may also want to bring along your video camera to record that "big" find, no matter what it might be.

Not pictured, but to be considered: knee pads and seat cushions.

Other Safety Precautions
- Never go into the field or on an unsupervised site alone. With protective clothing, reasonable care, proper use of equipment, and common sense,

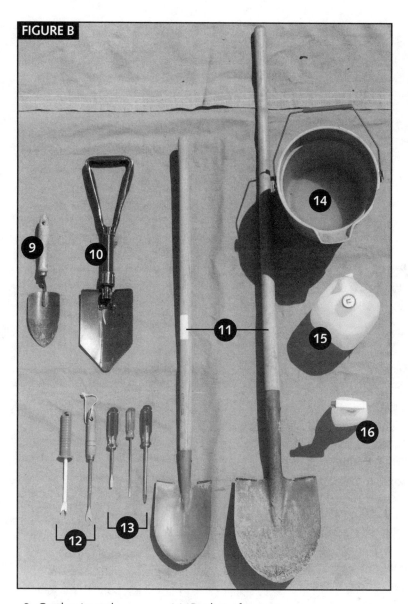

FIGURE B

9. Garden trowel
10. Camp shovel
11. Shovels
12. Garden cultivators
13. Screwdrivers

14. Bucket of water
15. (Plastic) jug of water
16. Squirt bottle of water; comes in handy at many of the mines to wash off rocks so you can see if they are or contain gem material

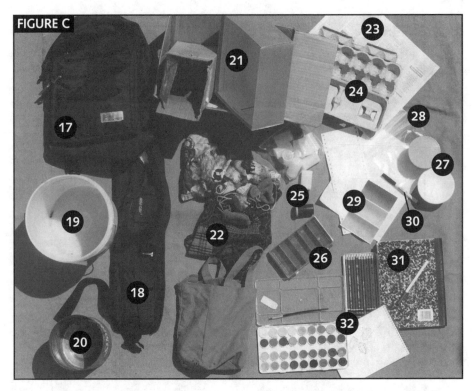

FIGURE C

17. Backpack
18. Waist pack to hold specimens
19. Bucket to hold specimens
20. Coffee can to hold specimens
21. Boxes to pack, transport, and ship specimens
22. Bags—various sized bags to carry collected specimens in the field
23. Newspaper to wrap specimens for transport
24. Egg cartons to transport delicate specimens
25. Empty film canisters to hold small specimens
26. Plastic box with dividers to hold small specimens
27. Margarine containers to hold small specimens

28. Reclosable plastic bags to hold small specimens
29. Gummed labels to label specimens (Whether you are at a fee dig site or with a guide, usually there will be someone to help you identify your find. It is a good idea to label the find when it is identified so that when you reach home, you won't have boxes of unknown rocks.)
30. Waterproof marker for labeling
31. Field log book to make notes on where specimens were found
32. Sketching pencils, sketchbook, paint to record your finds and the surrounding scenery

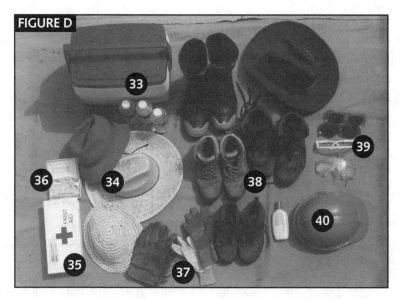

FIGURE D

33. Food and water—always carry plenty of drinking water (*Note:* many sites tell you in advance if they have food and water available or if you should bring some; however, it is always a good idea to bring extra drinking water. Remember—if you bring it in, pack it back out.)

34. Hats. Many of the sites are in the open, and the summer sun can be hot and dangerous to unprotected skin. Check with the site to see if they have any recommendations for protective clothing. Also, don't forget sunscreen.

35. First aid/safety kit

36. Snakebite kit. If the area is known to have snakes, be alert and take appropriate safety measures, such as boots and long pants. (*Note:* while planning our first gem-hunting trip, we read that the first aid kit should contain a snakebite kit. Just like rockhounds, snakes seem to love rocky areas!) In most cases, if you visit sites in the book, you will be either at a flume provided by the facility, or with an experienced guide. At the first, you will most likely never see a snake; at the second, your guide will fill you in on precautions. For listings where you will be searching on a ranch or state park, ask about special safety concerns such as snakes and insects when you pay your fee. These sites may not be for everyone.

37. Gloves to protect your hands when you are working with sharp rock or using a hammer or chisel

38. Boots—particularly important at sites where you will be doing a lot of walking, or walking on rocks

39. Safety glasses with side shields, or goggles. Particularly important at hard rock sites or any site where you or others may be hitting rocks. Safety glasses are available with tinted lenses for protection from the sun.

40. Hard hats—may be mandatory if you are visiting an active quarry or mine; suggested near cliffs

accidents should be avoided, but in the event of an illness or accident, you always want to have someone with you who can administer first aid and call for or seek help.

- Always keep children under your supervision.
- Never enter old abandoned mines or underground diggings!
- Never break or hammer rocks close to another person!

Mining Techniques

How to Sluice for Gems

This is the most common technique used at fee dig mines where you buy a bucket of gem ore (gem dirt) and wash it at a flume.

1. Place a quantity of the gem ore in the screen box, and place the screen box in the water. Use enough gem ore to fill the box about a third.

2. Place the box in the water, and shake it back and forth, raising one side,

Clockwise from top: Gold pan; screen box used for sluicing; screen box used for screening.

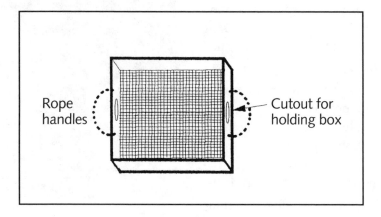

Rope handles

Cutout for holding box

How to Build a Screen Box

1. A screen box that is easy to handle is generally built from 1" x 4" lumber and window screening.

2. Decide on the dimensions of the screen box you want, and cut the wood accordingly. Dimensions generally run from 12" x 12" up to 18" x 18". Remember that the end pieces will overlap the side pieces, so cut the end pieces 1½" longer.

3. There are two alternative methods of construction. In one, drill pilot holes in the end pieces, and use wood screws to fasten the end pieces to the side pieces. In the other, use angle irons and screws to attach the ends and sides.

4. Cut the screening to be ¼" smaller than the outside dimensions of the screen box, and use staples to attach the screen to the bottom of the box. Use metal screening rather than plastic if possible. For a stronger box, cut ¼" or ⅜" hardware cloth to the same dimensions as the screening, and staple the hardware cloth over the screening. The hardware cloth will provide support for the screening.

5. Cut ¼" wood trim to fit, and attach it to the bottom of the box to cover the edges of the screening and hardware cloth and staples.

6. If you like, add rope handles or cut handholds in the side pieces for easier handling.

then the other, so that the material in the box moves back and forth. What you are doing is making the stones move around in the screen box, while washing dirt and sand out of the mixture.

3. After a minute or two of washing, take the screen box out of the flume, and let it drain. Look through the stones remaining in the screen box for your treasure. If you're not sure about something, ask one of the attendants.

4. When you can't finding anything more, put the box back in the flume and wash it some more, then take it out and search again.

5. If possible, move your screen box into bright light while you are searching, since the gems and minerals often show up better in bright light.

How to Screen for Gems

This is another common technique used at fee dig mines where you buy a bucket of gem ore and screen it for gems. (The authors used this technique for garnets and sapphires in Montana.)

1. Place a quantity of the gem ore in the screen box, and place the screen box in the water. Use enough gem dirt to fill the box about a third.

2. Place the box in the water, and begin tipping it back and forth, raising one side, then the other, so that the material in the box moves back and forth. What you are doing is making the gemstones, which are heavier than the rock and dirt, move into the bottom center of the screen box while at the same time washing dirt and sand out of the mixture.

3. After a minute or two, change the direction of movement to front and back.

4. Repeat these two movements (Steps 2 and 3) three or four times.

5. Take the box out of the water and let it drain, then place a board on top and carefully flip the box over onto the sorting table. It may be helpful to

put a foam pad in the box, then put the board over it. This helps keep the stones in place when you flip the box. If you have done it right, the gemstones will be found in the center of the rocks dumped onto the board. Use tweezers to pick the rough gemstones out of the rocks, and place them in a small container.

How to Pan for Gold

The technique for panning for gold is based on the fact that gold is much heavier than rock or soil. Gently washing and swirling the gold-bearing soil in a pan causes the gold to settle to the bottom of the pan. A gold pan has a flat bottom and gently slanting sides. Some modern pans also have small ridges or rings around the inside of the pan on these slanting sides. As the soil is washed out of the pan, the gold will slide down the sides, or be caught on the ridges and stay in the pan. Here's how:

1. Begin by filling the pan with ore, about ⅔ to ¾ full.

2. Put your pan in the water, let it gently fill with water, then put the pan under the water surface. Leave the pan in the water, and mix the dirt around in the pan, cleaning and removing any large rocks.

3. Lift the pan out of the water, then gently shake the pan from side to side while swirling it at the same time. Do this for 20–30 seconds to get the gold settled to the bottom of the pan.

4. Still holding the pan out of the water, continue these motions while tilting the pan so that the dirt begins to wash out. Keep the angle of the pan so that the crease (where the bottom and sides meet) is the lowest point.

5. When there is only about a tablespoon of material left in the pan, put about ½ inch of water in the pan, and swirl the water over the remaining material. As the top material is moved off, you should see gold underneath.

6. No luck? Try again at a different spot.

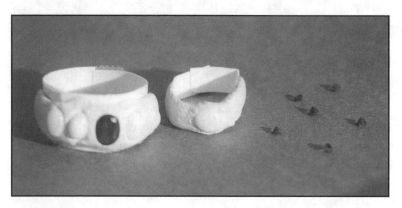

The authors sent their rough gems away for faceting. Using the faceted gems, they made crude mock-ups and sketches of the rings they wanted; then they sent the mock-ups, sketches, and gems to be made into rings.

The finished rings.

Notes on Gem Faceting, Cabbing, and Mounting Services

Many of the fee dig sites offer services to cut and mount your finds. Quality and costs vary. Trade journals such as *Lapidary Journal* and *Rock & Gem* (available at most large bookstores or by subscription) list suppliers of these services, both in the United States and overseas. Again, quality and cost vary. Local rock and gem shops in your area may offer these services, or it may be possible to work with a local jeweler. Your local rock club may be able to provide these services or make recommendations.

After their first gem-hunting trip, the authors had some of their finds faceted and cabochoned. They then designed rings and had them made using these stones, as shown in the photos on the previous page.

Taking sifted gravel to the jig at a sapphire mine in Montana. Pictured from left to right: Steve, Kathy, Annie Rygle, Debra Pedersen, Kristin Pedersen.

ALASKA

State Gemstone: Jade (1968)
State Mineral: Gold (1968)

FAIRBANKS / *Easy*

Pan for Gold *T*

The following gems or minerals may be found:

▪ Gold

El Dorado Gold Mine
1975 Discovery Drive
Fairbanks, AK 99709
Phone: (907) 479-6673; (866) 479-6673
Fax: (907) 479-4613
E-mail: reservations@eldoradogoldmine.
com

Open: Mid-May–mid-September. Tours depart 9:45 A.M. and 3:00 P.M. daily (no morning tours Monday or Saturday).

Info: After a short "course" on mining, try your hand at panning for gold. Gold panning is included in the El Dorado Gold Mine tour. See Section 2 for more information on the mine tour.

Rates: "Pokes" of pay dirt are provided as part of the tour. See listing under Section 2.

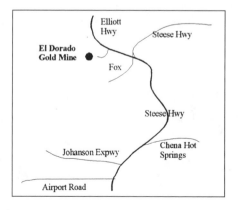

Other services available: Ride a narrow-gauge railroad through the past to a working gold mine; walking tour of mining camp; large gold nugget display; airstrip.

Directions: Nine miles north of Fairbanks on the Elliott Highway. Located on Highway #2 off Elliott Highway.

FAIRBANKS / *Easy*

Pan for Gold *T*

The following gems or minerals may be found:

▪ Gold

Gold Dredge No. 8
1755 Old Steese Highway North
Fairbanks, AK 99712
Phone: (907) 457-6058
Fax: (907) 457-8888
www.golddredgeno8.com

Open: Mid-May–mid-September, 9:00 A.M.–6:00 P.M., daily

Info: As part of the tour of Gold Dredge No. 8, pan gold just like a real Alaskan prospector. You are guaranteed to find gold during your panning experience. The water is heated, so your hands won't get too cold. For further information on the Gold Dredge tour, see the listing in Section 2.

Features: Pan for gold. Pans, shovels, and hands-on guidance are provided.

Keep what you find; have it weighed at the "Assay Office."

Rates: Gold panning is provided as part of the tour. See listing under Section 2.

Other services available: Dining hall with miner's stew; museums and warehouse exhibits.

Directions: North on Steese Highway to Goldstream Road. Turn left on Goldstream Road to Old Steese Highway. Turn left on Old Steese Highway to the Gold Dredge. Map available on website.

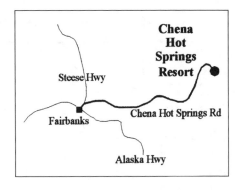

FAIRBANKS / *Easy*

Pan for Gold

The following gems or minerals may be found:

- Gold

Chena Hot Springs Resort
P.O. Box 58740
Fairbanks, AK 99711
Phone: (907) 451-8104;
(800) 478-4681 (U.S.)
Fax: (907) 456-3122
www.chenahotsprings.com

Open: Contact the resort for details of when panning is available.

Panning fee: Sack of pay dirt $20.00.

Info: Chena Hot Springs was discovered in 1905 by gold prospectors seeking to ease their painful rheumatism brought on by poor diet and grueling work. By 1912, Chena Hot Springs had become the premier resort of Interior Alaska, a mere 1- to 3-week trip by stagecoach from Fairbanks. Today it is only a 75-minute drive from Fairbanks.

The hot springs are located at the center of a 40-square-mile geothermal resource area. Water from the hot springs is 156°F and must be cooled before bathers can take advantage of its invigorating properties.

Other services available: Resort, lodge, and cabins; hiking trails; horseback riding; viewing northern lights; viewing wildlife; mountain biking, fishing, and rafting; cross-country skiing; snowmobiling; sleigh rides; snow coach tours; dog mushing; tent sites; RV parking; picnic sites.

Directions: From Fairbanks, take Steese Highway north to Chena Hot Springs Road. Follow Chena Hot Springs Road to the resort.

ANCHORAGE

Museum

Gem Museum
c/o Stewart's Photo Shop
Mrs. Oro Stewart
531 W. 4th Avenue
Anchorage, AK 99501
Phone: (907) 272-8581 (shop); (907) 277-2931 (home)

Open: By appointment.
Info: Gem and mineral displays. Information is available on Alaskan and international rockhounding tours. Oro Stewart's husband was an Alaskan jade miner.
Admission: Free.
Directions: The shop is located on West 4th Avenue in Anchorage.
Note: Kids—ask Mrs. Stewart about her pet reindeer named Star, who likes apples.

FAIRBANKS

Mine Tour

El Dorado Gold Mine
1975 Discovery Drive
Fairbanks, AK 99701
Phone: (907) 479-6673; (866) 479-6673
Fax: (907) 479-4613
E-mail: reservations@eldoradogoldmine.com

Open: Mid-May–mid-September. Tours depart 9:45 A.M. and 3:00 P.M. daily (no morning tours Monday or Saturday).
Info: Reservations and prepayment required. The tour begins with a ride on an authentic narrow-gauge railroad through the past to a working gold mine. The local miners will explain mining, past and present. You pass through a permafrost tunnel and learn of the conditions miners faced working in the Arctic terrain. You can also view a large gold nugget display. The trip takes approximately 2 hours.
Tour fee: Adults $27.95 (includes tour of mine), children 3–12 $19.95, children under 3 free.
Directions: 9 miles north of Fairbanks on the Elliott Highway. Tours depart from the old train station at 1.3 miles on Elliott Highway, just past Fox.

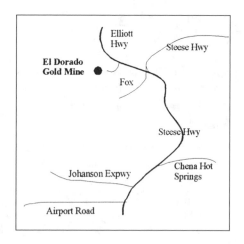

Mining Dredge Tour

Gold Dredge No. 8
Fairbanks, AK 99712
Phone: (907) 457-6058
Fax: (907) 457-8888
www.golddredgeno8.com

Open: Mid-May–Mid-September 9:00 A.M.–6:00 P.M. Tours starting every hour on the half hour from 9:30 A.M. to 3:30 P.M. daily.

Info: Tour Alaska's mining history. This is Alaska's only gold dredge open to the public. See the historic dredge, bunkhouse, dining hall, and warehouse—an opportunity to see how millions of ounces of gold were recovered from the Goldstream Valley. The tour includes video and walk down Fairbanks Creek Camp, guided tour through Gold Dredge No. 8, and gold panning. The museums and warehouse exhibits can be explored at your leisure.

Admission: Adults $23.00, children 6–12 $18.00 (includes tour of dredge and panning). Group rates are available.

A hearty miners' stew is available from 11:00 A.M. to 3:00 P.M. in the dining hall: $9.50 for adults, $7.50 for children 6–12.

Directions: North on Steese Highway to Goldstream Road. Turn left on Goldstream Road to Old Steese Highway. Turn left on Old Steese Highway to the Gold Dredge.

Museum

University of Alaska Museum
907 Yukon Drive
P.O. Box 756960
Fairbanks, AK 99775-6960
Phone: (907) 474-7505
Fax: (907) 474-5469
www.uaf.alaska.edu/museum

Open: All year. May 15–September 15, 9:00 A.M.–7:00 P.M. September 16–May 14, 9:00 A.M.–5:00 P.M. weekdays, noon–5:00 P.M. weekends.

Info: The Geology Department's collection includes excellent examples of minerals and gems from Alaska and the Pacific Rim, ore samples from Alaska and Arctic Canada, outstanding placer gold fines and nuggets, and meteorites.

A series of plate tectonic maps in the southeast gallery shows the reconstruction of Alaska's geologic history.

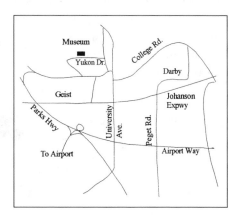

There is an outdoor exhibit of a mining stamp mill.

Admission: Adults $5.00, seniors $4.50, youth (13–18) $3.00, children under 6 free.

Other services available: Museum store.

Directions: The museum is located at 970 Yukon Drive on the University of Alaska–Fairbanks campus.

SECTION 3: Special Events and Tourist Information

TOURIST INFORMATION

Field Trips

Chugah Gem & Mineral Society
Box 92027
Anchorage, AK 99509-2027

Info: If you're visiting Alaska, contact the Chugah Gem & Mineral Society about field trips. If you are from out of town, you can subscribe to their monthly newsletter "Alaska Pebble Patter" for $10.00. The newsletter includes information on local and international field trips as well as interesting and relevant articles.

Directions: Contact the Society for directions.

State Tourist Agency

Alaska Division of Tourism
P.O. Box 110809
Juneau, AK 99811-0809
Phone: (907) 465-2017
Fax: (907) 465-3767
www.state.ak.us

Fairbanks Convention & Visitors Bureau
550 First Avenue
Fairbanks, AK 99701
Phone: (800) 327-5774; (907) 456-5774
Fax: (907) 452-4190

IDAHO

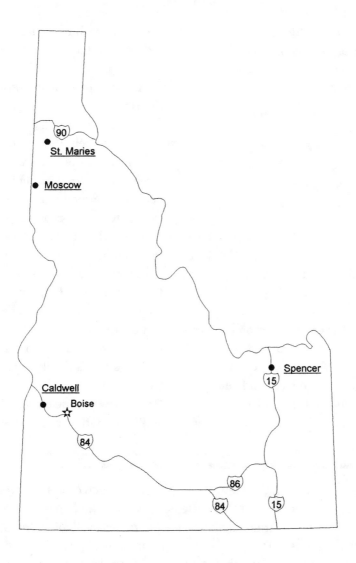

State Gemstone: Star Garnet (1967)

MOSCOW / *Native • Moderate to Difficult*

Licensed Guide for Star Garnet Digging *T*

The following gems or minerals may be found:

- **Star Garnets**

3-D's Panhandle Gems and Garnet
Queen Mine
Louise Darby
P.O. Box 9082
Moscow, ID 83843
Phone: (208) 882-9496

Open: Memorial Day weekend–Labor Day, 9:00 A.M.–5:00 P.M. Closed Wednesdays and Thursdays. Call for open sign-up dates.

All trips must be booked in advance; 30 days advance notice recommended; prepaid reservation required.

Info: Licensed guide service to garnet-digging activities on land in Idaho Panhandle National Forest. Idaho is one of only two locations in the world where star garnets can be found. The garnet area is located in the east and west forks of 281 draw. There is a ¾-mile walk uphill to get to the area. The east fork trip is not recommended if you have mobility problems, since the slope is very steep.

All equipment and instruction are furnished. Visitors learn where to look for star garnets, how they were formed, and how to tell a star garnet from a facet-grade garnet. Bring your own lunch, drink, and container for your garnets, and transportation to the site. Old clothes, tennis shoes or lace boots, and a change of clothing from the waist down are recommended; rubber boots are not, since they are slippery when wet.

Fee: $65.00 per adult, $50.00 per child 13 and under. Fee includes $10.00 National Forest Service fee and $5.00 user fee, as well as Idaho sales tax. Private trips are also available for groups of 5 or more.

Other services available: Wholesale and retail outlet specializing in Idaho

Idaho's nickname is the Gem State. Although much of Idaho's wealth of gems and minerals is in remote areas, to be searched only by the hardiest of rockhounds, there are some fee dig mines available. One of them is in an area that is one of only two locations in the world where star garnets can be found. The other is a location for collecting fire opals.

star garnet, custom jewelry design, polishing, casting, cutting, and repairs. You can have your garnet cut and polished at the lapidary shop.

Louise Darby also offers an 8-day tour of northern Idaho which includes a 3-day whitewater raft trip on the Salmon River, where you will hear tales of gold and do some panning for gold yourself.

Directions: By appointment only. To the shop (1226 Juliene Way): East on Highway 8, turn right at milepost marker No. 7. Turn left and stop at the second place on the left.

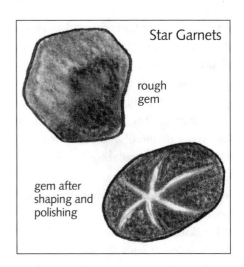

Star Garnets

rough gem

gem after shaping and polishing

SPENCER / *Native • Easy to Difficult*

Dig Your Own 𝑇

The following gems or minerals may be found:

- **Precious opal**

Spencer Opal Mine
HC 62, Box 2060
Spencer, ID 83446
Phone: (208) 374-5476 (May–September)
P.O. Box 521
Salome, AZ 85348
Phone: (928) 859-3752 (October–April)

Open: Mine shop is open 7 days/week, May–October. Fee dig at mine holiday weekends; vary each year, call for dates. Groups of 20 or more can fee dig with prior reservations.

Info: Dig your own opal at a "mini-mine" at the headquarters shop in a large stockpile of mine run ore. Public digging is allowed at the mine on holiday weekends. Groups may be allowed at the mine with a minimum of 2 weeks' advance registration.

The primary formation of the mine is a rhyolite and obsidian flow full of gas pockets. The opal solution, or silica, was a secondary deposit carried by geyser activity. As a result of several eruptions over time, the opal lies in layers. Most of the layers are thin, resulting in what has been said to be some of the most beautiful triplet opal in the world. Occasionally the layer will be thick enough for cutting a solid opal—a bonus for the finder.

Digging at the actual mine involves breaking rock. A rock hammer and sledgehammer are needed. Bring a spray bottle with water to clean the rock and look for color in the opal. Safety precautions for breaking rock should be followed. Wear safety glasses. Sunscreen and a sun-hat are recommended, as are long pants and hard-sided shoes or boots.

Admission: For "mini-mine": Adults $5.00 includes 1 pound of rock; $5.00 per pound of additional rock collected. For mine: $30.00, dig up to 5 pounds; $5.00 per pound of additional rock.

Other services available: The shop carries a full line of opal cutting supplies, as well as rough and finished stones and jewelry.

Directions: Spencer is located on I-15 in southeastern Idaho, 63 miles north of Idaho Falls, 30 miles south of Dillon, Montana, and 70 miles west of Yellowstone National Park. The headquarters shop is located at the north end of Main Street in Spencer, at the gas station and Opal Country Cafe.

ST. MARIES / *Native • Moderate to Difficult*

Dig and Wash Gravel *T*

The following gems or minerals may be found:

- **Star garnets, garnets**

Emerald Creek Garnet Area
St. Joe Ranger District
P.O. Box 407
St. Maries, Idaho 83861
Phone: (208) 245-2531
Fax: (208) 245-6052
www.recreation.gov; www.palouse.net (choose "Countryside" then "Emerald Creek")

Open: West fork, 281 Gulch, Memorial Day through Labor Day; East fork, early July through Labor Day. 9:00 A.M.–5:00 P.M., Friday–Tuesday.

Info: Northern Idaho and India are the two places in the world where star garnets are found. The 12-sided (dodecahedron) crystals range from sand-particle size to golf-ball size or larger, and are often found with four- or six-ray stars. Gem-quality faceting material is also found.

A permit is required for anyone digging, screening, or washing gravel. A permit allows you to dig in a designated area only. Up to 5 pounds of garnets may be taken under a daily permit. If you want to remove more garnets during the same day, you can buy another daily permit for an additional 5 pounds or fraction thereof. The limit is 6 permits or 30 pounds of garnet per year.

Daily Permit Fee: Adults $10.00, children under 14 $5.00

Assistance provided to garnet diggers; bring your own tools, or rent at $1.00 each.

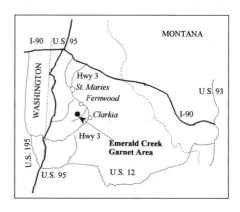

Star Garnets

The star effect is a defect in the garnet. Also called asterism, it results from minute needles of rutile (titanium dioxide), which are found in the structure of the garnet. When light is focused on the garnet, the needles reflect it back onto the surface, causing the star. If the needles are facing in two directions, the result is a four-ray star; if the needles are facing in three directions, the result is a six-ray star. While four-ray stars are found in Idaho and in India, six-ray star garnets have been found only in Idaho.

Digging for Star Garnets

To find star garnets, you have to dig from 1–10 feet deep. Garnets are generally found in alluvial deposits of gravel and sand just above bedrock, or in mica schist parent material.

Equipment needed:

- Rubber boots, waders, or old tennis shoes
- Change of clothes—garnet digging is wet, muddy work
- Standard shovel
- Bucket for bailing water
- Container for garnets—a 1-pound coffee can will hold 5 pounds of garnets
- Screen box for washing gravel

Other services available: Restrooms; displays; pets are allowed on a leash.

Nearby accommodations: Emerald Creek Campground is 4 miles east. Campground fee is $6.00/night. This is also the location of the nearest safe drinking water. Nearest motels are in St. Marie (30 miles). Clarkia Bunkhouse Kitchen (208-245-1134) has rooms with shared showers. Food, gas, and other supplies are available in Clarkia (6 miles), Fernwood (12 miles), and Emida (25 miles). Laundromats are in Fernwood and St. Maries.

Directions: From St. Maries, follow Highway 3 south 24 miles to Road 447. Proceed southwest 8 miles on Road 447 to the parking area. Permits, information, and the digging area are a ½-mile hike up 281 Gulch. (Carry your equipment with you.)

SECTION 2: Museums and Mine Tours

CALDWELL

Museum 🏛

The Glen L. and Ruth M. Evans Gem
and Mineral Collection
Orma J. Smith Museum of Natural
History
The College of Idaho
2112 Cleveland Boulevard
Caldwell, ID 83605
Phone: (208) 459-5301
www.albertson.edu

Open: When college is in session, after-noons on school days, and first Saturday of month (not conflicting with national holidays).
Info: Glen and Ruth Evans presented the College of Idaho with a spectacular collection, which includes 52 glass-enclosed cases in two rooms containing Brazilian and Mexican agate, Biggs jasper, variscite, Lake Superior agate, tiger eye, Bruneau jasper, Owyhee jasper, and many other gemstones.

Two revolving cases contain over 2,000 cabochons, or "cabs," made from all varieties of materials, some no longer available. Spheres of all sizes and materials number in the hundreds. Also included are carved jade from Taiwan, corals from the Pacific islands, fluorescent minerals, and native gold and silver in various forms from Idaho mines. One display contains many mineral crystals, unpolished, just as they occur in nature. The collection contains gems from all sectors of the US and from many coun-tries. Ruth Evans faceted, cut, and polished many of the specimens. All items in the col-lection are descriptively labeled.

The collection is located on the main floor of the William Judson Boone Hall (Science Center).

The museum is the home of extensive collections of minerals. It is located in the basement of the Boone Science Center.
Admission: Free.
Directions: On the college campus in Caldwell, Idaho.

SECTION 3: Special Events and Tourist Information

TOURIST INFORMATION

State Tourist Agency

Idaho Travel Council Administrative Office
Idaho Department of Commerce
700 West State Street

P.O. Box 83720
Boise, ID 83720-0093
Phone: (800) 842-5858; (208) 334-2470
Fax: (208) 334-2631
www.visitid.org

IOWA

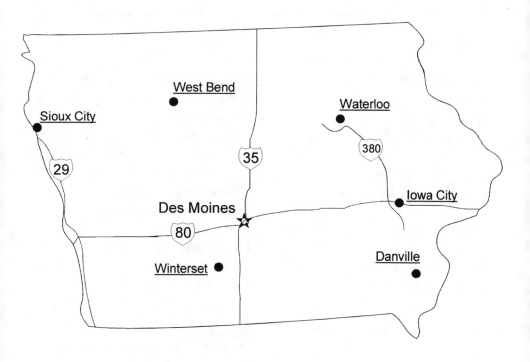

West Bend

Waterloo

Sioux City

380

35

Des Moines

29

Iowa City

80

Danville

Winterset

State Stone/Rock: Geode

SECTION 1: Fee Dig Sites and Guide Services

No information available.

SECTION 2: Museums and Mine Tours

DANVILLE

Museum
Geode State Park
3249 Racine Avenue
Danville, IA 52623
Phone: (319) 392-4601
Fax: (319) 392-4605
E-mail: geode@dnr.state.ia.us

Open: All year round, weather permitting, 4 A.M.–10:30 P.M.; 7 days a week.
Info: The park is named for the geode stones which rockhounds hunt in this area. A display of geodes with a variety of mysterious crystal formations can be found at the park campground.
Note: *It is illegal to remove geodes from the state park.*

Not far across the state line in Missouri is a fee dig location for geodes. See the listing under Alexandria, Missouri.
Admission: Call for rates.
Directions: Geode State Park can be reached from U.S. 34, which goes between Burlington and Mt. Pleasant. Take State Highway 79 from U.S. 34 to get to the park.

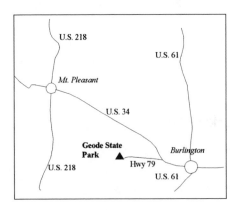

IOWA CITY

Museum
The University of Iowa
Museum of Natural History
10 Macbride Hall
Iowa City, IA 52242
Phone: (319) 335-0481
Fax: (319) 335-0653
www.uiowa.edu

Open: Monday–Saturday, 9:30 A.M.–4:30 P.M.; Sunday, 12:30–4:30 P.M. Closed university holidays.

Admission: Free.

Info: Iowa Hall contains over 60 exhibits about the history of Iowa. Take a walk through the 5-billion year story of the state's geology.

Directions: The University of Iowa is located in Iowa City just off U.S. 218, 6 miles south of I-80.

SIOUX CITY

Museum

Sioux City Public Museum
2901 Jackson Street
Sioux City, IA 51104-3697
Phone: (712) 279-6174
Fax: (712) 252-5615
E-mail: scpm@sioux-city.org
www.sioux-city.org/museum

Open: Tuesday 9:00 A.M.–8:00 P.M., Wednesday–Saturday 9:00 A.M.–5:00 P.M., Sunday 1:00–5:00 P.M.

Info: Exhibits in mineralogy explain the various properties and characteristics of minerals as well as their chemical compatibilities and possible commercialization.

Admission: Free.

Directions: Located in Sioux City, on Jackson Street.

WATERLOO

Museum

Grout Museum of History and Science
503 South Street
Waterloo, IA 50701
Phone: (319) 234-6357
Fax: (319) 236-0500

Open: Tuesday–Saturday 10:00 A.M.–4:30 P.M.; Sunday 1:00–4:30 P.M.

Info: The museum has two permanent cases displaying rocks and minerals in the main level of the museum. The hands-on children's space, the Discovery Zone, has Discovery Boxes featuring rocks, minerals, and fossils.

Admission: Adults $3.50, children 3–12 $2.50, children under 3 free.

Directions: On South Street between Park Avenue and West 4th, one block south of Highway 218.

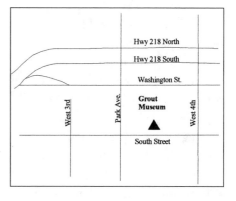

WEST BEND

Grotto 🏛

Grotto of the Redemption
West Bend, IA 50597
Phone: (515) 887-2371
Fax: (515) 887-2372
E-mail: grotto@ncn.net

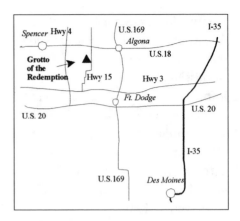

Open: Daily tours May 1–October 15 or by appointment, 10:00 A.M.–5:00 P.M. 7 days/week. Museum and grotto are open to visitors all year. Group tours by appointment. Tours can be arranged earlier in the spring.

Info: The grotto is a composite of nine separate grottos, each portraying some scene in the life of Christ. It is said to include the largest collection of precious stones and gems found anywhere in one location and is the largest grotto in the world. The grotto is said to have an estimated geological value of $2,500,000. Guided tours take approximately 1 hour and include a geological lecture in the Rock Display Studio.

The Grotto Museum includes a large display of precious and semiprecious stones from throughout the world. The grotto is flooded with spotlights for evening viewing. The church is open to the public for visits to the Christmas Chapel.

Admission: Suggested donation: $5.00 adults, $2.50 children.

Other services available: The gift store is open from April–December. A restaurant is available at the Grotto. The campground offers overnight camping, including showers and electrical hookups. Fees are $10.00 for campers, $5.00 for tents.

Directions: Take State Highway 15 south from U.S. 18 (which goes between Spencer and Algona). The grotto is on Highway 15 just outside of West Bend, approximately 8 miles from U.S. 18.

WINTERSET

Museum 🏛

Madison County Historical Society
815 South 2nd Avenue
Winterset, IA 50273
Phone: (515) 462-2134
www.plantnet.com/museum.html

Open: May 1–October 31, Monday–Saturday 11:00 A.M.–4:00 P.M., Sunday 1:00–5:00 P.M.

Info: An extensive collection of rocks and minerals donated by Amel Priest is displayed. Amel, who farmed 400 acres near Peru, developed an interest in collecting rocks, minerals, and fossils in response to the curiosity of his Boy Scout troop. He added to his collection by trading the fossils he found for minerals and rocks from around the world. (Some of Priest's fossils were donated to the Smithsonian Institution in Washington, DC.)

Admission: $3.00

Directions: Winterset can be reached by traveling south on U.S. 169 from Exit 110 on I-80 or by traveling west on State Highway 92 from Exit 56 on I-35. 2nd Avenue is two blocks west of U.S. 169.

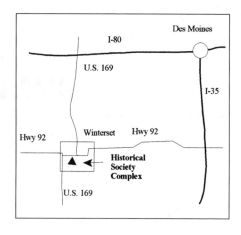

SECTION 3: Special Events and Tourist Information

TOURIST INFORMATION

State Tourist Agency

Iowa Department of Economic
Development
Iowa Tourism Office
200 East Grand Avenue
Des Moines, IA 50309
Phone: (515) 242-4705; (888) 472-6035
Fax: (515) 242-4718
www.traveliowa.com

MINNESOTA

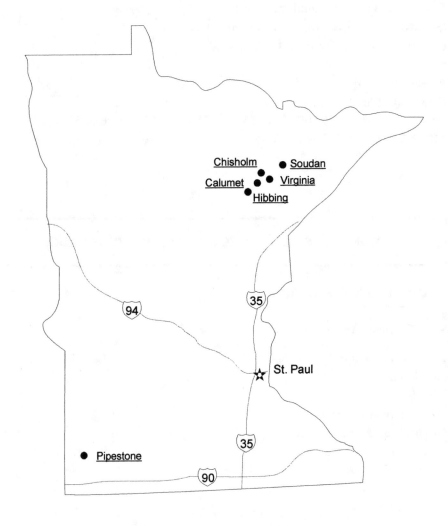

State Gemstone: Lake Superior Agate

SECTION 1: Fee Dig Sites and Guide Services

No information available.

SECTION 2: Museums and Mine Tours

CALUMET

Mine Tour

Hill Annex Mine State Park
Minnesota Department of Natural
Resources
P.O. Box 376
Calumet, MN 55716
Phone: (218) 247-7215
www.DNR.state.mn.us

Open: Weekdays 9:00 A.M.–4:00 P.M.
Memorial Day–Labor Day 8:00 A.M.–
6:00 P.M. Bus tours 10:00 A.M.–2:00 P.M.,
leave on the hour. Mine boat tours daily
at 3:30 P.M.

Info: One and a half hour tour of the
open-pit Hill Annex Iron Mine. Learn
about how the mine operated, the people who worked in the mine, and their
origins. Learn about the role this mine
played in state, national, and world history. Two-hour adventure aboard a pon-
toon boat that tours one of Minnesota's
most productive open pit iron ore mines.
Admission: Adults $6.00, children 5–12
$4.00.

Directions: On U.S. 169 between Grand
Rapids and Hibbing.

** See our upcoming sequel on fossils
for fossil hunting tours at this site.*

CHISHOLM

Mining Displays 🏛

Ironworld Discovery Center
HWY 169 West
P.O. Box 392
Chisholm, MN 55719
Phone: (218) 254-7959; (800) 372-6437
www.ironworld.com

Open: May–September 9:30 A.M.–5:00 P.M.

Info: Learn about Minnesota's iron mining Industry. Park includes an old-time electric trolley, tours, climb-on equipment displays, exhibits, living history exhibits, concerts, and ethnic meals. The Iron Ore Miner Statue is located across from the park, paying tribute to all the men who worked in the early ore mines.

Admission: Adults $8.00, seniors $7.00, students (7–17) $6.00, children 6 and under free, family $24.00. Call for special spring and fall rates.

Other services available: The Iron Range Research Library and Archives contain one of the largest collections of genealogical and local history research material in the upper Midwest. Contact center for hours.

Directions: On U.S. 169 between Virginia and Hibbing.

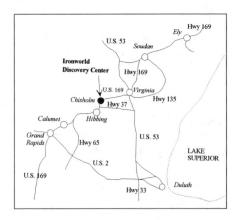

CHISHOLM

Museum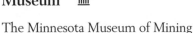

The Minnesota Museum of Mining
P.O. Box 271
Chisholm, MN 55719
Phone: (218) 254-5543

Open: Memorial Day–Labor Day, 9:00 A.M.–5:00 P.M.; 7 days/week.

Info: Indoor and outdoor exhibits tell the story of the iron mining industry in northern Minnesota. The museum features a geological rock display, a replica of an underground drift mine, and an old mining town.

Admission: Adults $3.00, seniors $2.50, students 5–17 $2.00, families $9.00.

Directions: In Memorial Park, at the top of Chisholm's Main Street.

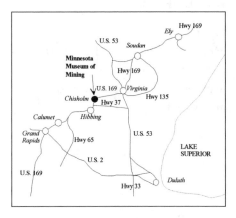

CHISHOLM

Mine Tour 🏛

Taconite Mine Tours
c/o Ironworld Discovery Center
P.O. Box 392
Chisholm, MN 55716
Phone: (218) 254-3321; (800) 372-6437

Open: June–mid-August, Wednesday and Thursday. Tour leaves at noon.

Info: Taconite is a low-grade magnetic ore that is blasted from the earth, ground to a fine powder, separated with huge magnets, pelletized, and then shipped to steel mills. The Hibbing Taconite Co. is owned by Bethlehem Steel Corporation, Cleveland-Cliffs Inc., and Stelco, Inc.

Hibbing Taconite Co. is participating with Ironworld Discovery Center to offer guided tours. Slacks and comfortable shoes are recommended. Hard hats, safety glasses, and ear plugs will be furnished. The tours leave from the Ironworld Discovery Center.

Admission: $5.00/person. Children

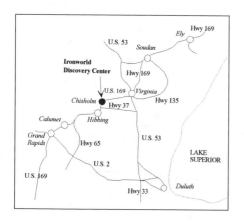

must be 10 or older and accompanied by an adult.

Directions: On U.S. 169 between Virginia and Hibbing.

HIBBING

Mine Tour 🏛

Mahoning Hull-Rust Mine
Tourist Center Seniors
1202 E. Howard Street
Hibbing, MN 55746
Phone: (218) 262-4166

Open: May 15–September 30, 9:00 A.M.–6:00 P.M., 7 days/week.

Info: The present Hull-Rust pit is reputed to be the largest open pit iron ore mine in the world. At 2,291 acres, it embraces more than 50 individual mines that were opened between 1895 and 1957. Since ore shipping began in 1895, more than 1.4 billion tons of earth have been removed from the mine. It has been called the Man-Made Grand Canyon of the North and is registered as a National Historic Site.

Attractions include mine observation stations and exterior mine exhibits.

Admission: Free.

Other services available: Walking trails; park and BBQ area.

Directions: On Third Avenue east in Hibbing. Take First Avenue north off US 169 to Howard Street. Take Howard Street east to Third Avenue. Take Third

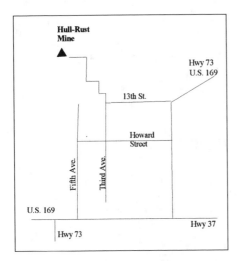

Avenue to the mine. From the north, travel south on U.S. 169 to 13th Street. Take 13th Street west to Third Avenue, then take Third Avenue north to the mine.

PIPESTONE

Quarry Tour 🏛

Pipestone National Monument
P.O. Box 727
Pipestone, MN 56164
Phone: (507) 825-3316; (507) 825-4126
www.nps.gov/pipe/

Open: All year, 8:00 A.M.–5:00 P.M. (longer in summer), 7 days/week.

Info: Stone pipes were long known among the prehistoric peoples of North America. Digging of pipestone at this Minnesota quarry likely began in the 17th century, a time that coincided with the acquisition of metal tools from European traders. Carvers prized this durable yet relatively soft stone, which ranges in color from mottled pink to brick red. By all accounts, this location came to be the preferred source of pipestone among the Plains tribes.

Pipecarving is by no means a lost art. Carvings today are appreciated as artwork as well as for their commemoration of history. The pipestone here may be quarried only by people of Native American ancestry.

Exhibits and a slide program at the visitors' center introduce the visitor to the history and cultural significance of this area. A ¾-mile self-guiding trail tours the quarry. The Upper Midwest Indian Cultural Center demonstrates the art of pipecarving.

Admission: Single visitor $3.00, vehicle entrance $5.00, both valid 7 days. Annual pass available for $15.00, which covers all immediate family members.

Directions: Pipestone National Monument is located at the junction of U.S. 75 and State Highway 30.

For information on other Native American stone quarries, see listings in

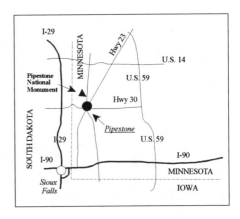

Newark, DE: jasper quarries (Vol. 4); Calumet and Copper Harbor, MI: copper (Vol. 4); Hopewell and Brownsville, OH: flint quarries (Vol. 4); and Fritch, TX: flint quarries (Vol. 2).

SOUDAN

Mine Tour 🏛

Soudan Underground Mine State Park
Minnesota Department of Natural Resources
Soudan, MN 55782
Phone: (218) 753-2245
E-mail: soudanmine@dnr.state.mn.us
www.dnr.state.mn.us/state_parks/soudan_underground_mine

Open: Daily public tours 10:00 A.M.–4:00 P.M. May 26–end of September. After that, call for schedule. Tours run on the hour. High energy Physics Tours also available.

Info: The Soudan Mine was Minnesota's first underground mine and is its deepest. The tour includes a 3-minute 2,400-foot elevator ride down to the 27th level (½ mile underground), an electric train ride through a tunnel ¾ mile long, and a tour of the last and deepest area mined. A self-guided surface tour includes access to the ore crusher, the drill shop, and the head frame.

Note: The temperature of the mine is a constant 50°F; jackets and comfortable walking shoes are recommended.

Admission: Adults $7.00, children 5–12

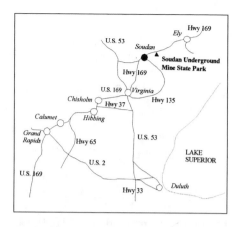

$5.00. Under 5 free. Vehicles entering the state park must have a MN state park pass; a 2-day pass is $4.00.

Other services available: Picnic area, hiking trails, snowmobile trails.

Directions: ½ mile north from Highway 169 along the shore of Lake Vermillion.

VIRGINIA

Mine View 🏛

Mineview in the Sky
Virginia Area Chamber of Commerce
P.O. Box 1072
Virginia, MN 55792
Phone: (218) 741-2717
www.irontrail.org

Open: May–September, 7 days/week.

Info: Mineview in the Sky overlooks the Rouchleau Mine and Rouchleau Group of Mines, an expanse of open pit mines that stretches nearly 3 miles in length and is a half mile wide. At its deepest point the mine is 450 feet deep. This group of mines

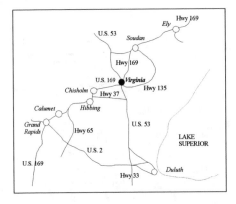

has produced more than 300,000,000 gross tons of iron ore. The mines were originally claimed by the Merritt brothers in the late 1800s. John D. Rockefeller ultimately acquired the Merritt holdings, and eventually the properties were transferred to the United States Steel Corp., which continues to hold an interest in the operation. The overlook was originally built as a vantage point for the pit supervisors to be able to view the entire operation; today, visitors can do the same.

Admission: Free.

Directions: East side of Highway 53, at the south end of Virginia.

VIRGINIA

Mine Views

Mine Views
c/o Iron Trail Convention & Visitors Bureau
403 North 1st Street
Virginia, MN 55792
Phone: (218) 749-8161; (800) 777-8497
E-mail: hcvb@cpinternet.com

Info: Many mine views are available in the area. Check with the Iron Trail Convention and Visitors Bureau for information and directions. The following are some of these mine views:

Mountain Iron Mine View

Open mid-May–September
Two sites in Mountain Iron provide views of the Minntac ore-taconite operations of U.S. Steel. One is located at the north end of Mountain Avenue; the second (called the Wacootah) is located on Highway 102.

Leonidas Overlook

Open mid-May–Labor Day
This overlook provides a spectacular panorama of the Eveleth Taconite Operations and the Minntac Mine. Located 1 mile west of Eveleth on County Highway 101.

Oldtown-Finntown Mine View

Open mid-May–September
Located in Virginia, this overlook offers a view of the Rocheleau Mine Group, reported to be the deepest mine in the area.

SECTION 3: Special Events and Tourist Information

TOURIST INFORMATION

State Tourist Agency

Minnesota Tourism Information
Office of Tourism
100 Metro Square
121 Seventh Place East
St. Paul, MN 55101
Phone: (651) 296-5029; (800) 657-3700
Fax: (651) 296-7095
E-mail: explore@state.mn.us
www.exploreminnesota.com

Minnesota State Parks

A vehicle permit ($4.00/day; $20.00/year) is required to enter and can be purchased at any park. Normal state park operating hours are 8:00 A.M.–10:00 P.M. For more information, call (866) 857-2757 or visit www.stayatmnparks.com.

Iron Trail Region

The Iron Trail region is set among the forests and lakes of northeastern Minnesota. The iron ore from the Mesabi range fed the nation's steel mills for more than half a century. Immigrants from more than 40 countries came to work in the mines and left behind colorful traditions, which continue today.

MONTANA

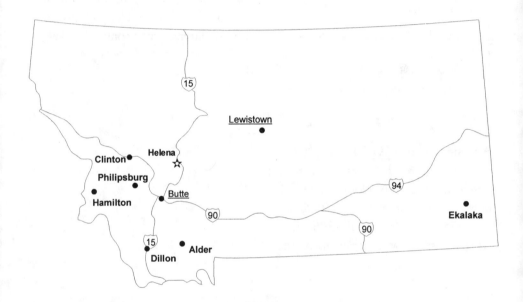

State Stone/Rock: Sapphire and Agate (1969)

ALDER / *Native · Easy*

Screen for Garnets *T*

The following gems or minerals may be found:

▪ **Garnets of varying colors, gold, sapphires**

Red Rock Mine
Steven Cox
Box 173
Alder, MT 59710
Phone: (406) 842-5378

Open: May 1–October 1, 9:00 A.M.–6:00 P.M. Monday–Saturday, 12:00–5:00 P.M. Sundays.

Info: Screen for garnets in concentrated gravel left over from a pond created by gold dredging. The garnets range in color from light pink to a deep blood red.

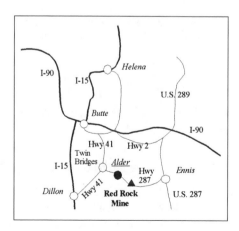

Some are of gem quality. Since this is part of the Ruby Valley, you may also find low-grade rubies. The mine supplies screen, water, pick, and shovel. You should bring gloves and sturdy shoes. For day digs, plan to bring a shade hat, gloves, sturdy shoes, lunch, and liquids.

Admission: Free, bucket $12.00, three buckets $30.00, sample bag $3.00, day digging in gravel pit $20.00 per adult for full day.

Also available are Montana gold, and Montana sapphire gravel, from other mines.

Other services available: Rock shop with gems, jewelry, rocks, and minerals; primitive bathrooms; picnic area; KOA campground with full facilities 1 mile west of mine.

Directions: 3 miles east of Alder on State Highway 287, between Alder and Ennis.

CLINTON / *Native ▪ Moderate to Difficult*

Sapphire Mining Pack Trip *T*

The following gems or minerals may be found:

▪ Sapphires of every color in the rainbow

L◊E Guest Ranch Outfitters
Dan or Retta Ekstrom
2421 Bonita R/S Road
Clinton, MT 59825
Phone: (406) 825-6295;
(888) PAK-TRIP (725-8747)

Open: End of June–mid-September.
Info: Travel by horseback approximately 11 miles from the trail head. The pack trip up to the mine includes breathtaking scenery, crossing mountain streams, and encountering wildlife. The Sapphire Camp is at a proven, registered claim, located in a high mountain meadow, with a spring-fed creek running through it. After mining during the day, enjoy a delicious camp-cooked meal, then relax around the campfire and discuss your finds. Accommodations are in 9' x 9' summer tents, with foam mattresses and an outdoor shower.
Rates: $200.00/day per person; 4-day minimum; 30% deposit required.
Other services available: Trout fishing; swimming; hunting; nature photography or trail riding.
Directions: The L◊E Ranch is located just off I-90, 25 miles east of Missoula and 85 miles west of Butte.

DILLON / *Native ▪ Moderate to Difficult*

Dig for Quartz and Amethyst Crystals *T*

The following gems or minerals may be found:

▪ Quartz crystals, and amethyst

Crystal Park Recreational Mineral Collecting Area
for information:

Dillon Ranger District Office
Beaverhead National Forest
420 Barrett Street
Dillon, MT 59725

Butte Mineral and Gem Club
P.O. Box 4492
Butte, MT 59702
Phone: (406) 683-3900

Open: May 15–September 30, daylight hours.
Info: The Butte Mineral and Gem Club maintains mining claims at Crystal Park and opens the claims to the public for digging. A host is usually available at Crystal Park to assist and to ensure rules are followed. About 30 acres of the 200 acres set aside for crystal digging are currently open. The digging area is a short walk from the paved parking area. The facilities are designed to be universally accessible. You must provide your own equipment and protective clothing.

Even in the hottest part of summer, a rain or snow shower can occur on any day at this high elevation. Also, bring a hand trowel, gardener's hand cultivator, gloves, a screen box with ¼" mesh, pack, sturdy shoes, hat, sunscreen, jacket, and insect repellent.

Note: Contact the U.S. Forest Service or Butte Mineral and Gem Club for digging tips and Crystal Park rules. Safe digging practices must be followed! Although digging is easy, because the decomposed granite is like coarse sand, it will cave in easily, quickly burying and suffocating anyone trapped under it. Be sure to follow the rules for safe digging: do not dig tunnels or deep steep-walled pits, or leave overhanging banks.

Rates: No fee is charged; donations for support of the operation and maintenance of the site are appreciated.

Other services provided: Three picnic areas with grills and toilets; a hand-operated water well; a paved walking trail with benches and an overlook; U.S. Forest Service campgrounds to the north and south of the park along the scenic byway.

Directions: From Butte, drive 3½ miles west on I-90 to the I-15 south exit. Drive 17 miles south on I-15 to the Divide exit. From Divide, travel 11 miles west on Highway 43 to Wise River. Just past Wise River, turn south on the Pioneer Mountains Scenic Byway and drive about 25 miles to Crystal Park. The roads are paved all the way.

From Dillon, drive 2½ miles south on I-15 to the Highway 278 exit, then 22 miles west on Highway 278 to the Pioneer Mountains Scenic Byway. Turn north at this intersection onto the Byway, and drive about 17 miles up the Grasshopper Creek Valley to Crystal Park. The Byway is gravel from Highway 278 to a mile south of Crystal Park.

HAMILTON / *Native • Moderate*

Search for Sapphires *T*

The following gems or minerals may be found:

▪ **Sapphires**

Sapphire Studio
P.O. Box 312
Hamilton, MT 59840
Phone: (406) 363-6650
E-mail: gems@sapphiremining.com
www.sapphiremining.com

Open: Call for times.

Info: Screen and search through bags of sapphire ore from their mine near Philipsburg, MT. Bags of dirt may be purchased at their store in Hamilton and screened there. In addition, the Sapphire Studio hosts occasional "Sapphire Fever" parties, where sapphire enthusiasts gather for an afternoon or evening of sapphire screening and camaraderie. During the event, videos of the mining operation are shown.

Admission: Free. Bags of sapphire ore $20.00.

Other services available: Gift shop; gem cutting.

Directions: Call for directions.

HELENA / *Native • Moderate*

Dig and Screen for Sapphires *T*

The following gems or minerals may be found:

• Sapphires, garnets, gold, hematite; topaz, quartz, ruby, jasper, agate, jadite, serpentine

Spokane Bar Sapphire Mine and Gold Fever Rock Shop
Russ and Deb Thompson
5360 Castles Drive
Helena, MT 59602
Phone: (406) 227-8989;
(877) DIG-GEMS (344-4367)
E-mail: Deb@sapphiremine.com
www.sapphiremine.com

Open: All year, 9:00 A.M.–5:00 P.M. (winter hours vary), 7 days/week.

Info: Bring your own equipment. Recommended tools include screwdriver, whiskbroom, tweezers, gloves, garden trowel, dustpan, and/or pick.

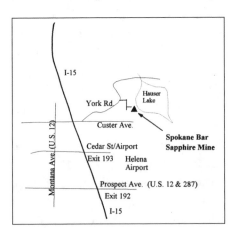

Admission: Free. Screen a 3½-gallon bucket of concentrate, $50.00. Dig a single 5-gallon bucket on hill and hand wash (screen), additional $10.00.

Other services available: Shop sells gemstones and mineral specimens, also prospecting tools. Concentrates may be ordered by UPS.

Directions: From Helena, take York Road to Mile Marker 8, turn right on Hart Lane. After road makes a 90° bend, turn left on Castles Road.

PHILIPSBURG / *Native • Moderate*

Search for Sapphires *T*

The following gems or minerals may be found:

• Sapphires

Gem Mountain
Chris Cooney
3835 Skalkaho Road
P.O. Box 148
Philipsburg, MT 59858
Phone: (406) 859-4367; (866) 459-4367
E-mail: info@gemmtn.com
www.gemmtn.com

Open: Call for times.

Info: Screen and search through bags of sapphire ore from their mine near Philipsburg, MT. Five-gallon buckets of dirt may be purchased and screened. Another option is to dig in mine dirt that has been hauled down from the mine, dry screen it by removing large

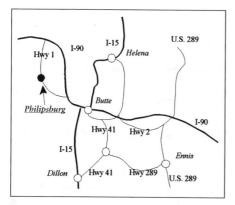

Search for Sapphires *T*

The following gems or minerals may be found:

- Sapphires

Sapphire Gallery
115 East Broadway
P.O. Box 2002
Philipsburg, MT 59858
Phone: (800) 525-0169
Fax: (406) 859-3631
www.sapphire-gallery.com

Open: All year, 10:00 A.M.–6:00 P.M. (summer), 10:00 A.M.–5:00 P.M. (winter), 6 days/week; closed Saturday.

Info: Visit the only all-sapphire store in the U.S., buy and wash bags of gravel in the store, and search for sapphires. When gravel is purchased and washed in the store, you are guaranteed to find a cuttable sapphire in a bag, or you will get another bag free.

The Victorian showroom, located in a Certified Historic Building, has a wide selection of sapphire jewelry.

Fee: Bag of gravel with one cut sapphire $25.00.

Other services available: Shop sells gems, fossils, and mineral specimens from around the world; goldsmithing services available; heat treating and faceting services available.

Directions: 115 East Broadway in Philipsburg.

rocks, and then search for sapphires.

Admission: Free. Bucket of sapphire ore $10.00. Dig your own: Admission $10.00, each bucket of screened ore $5.00. Jug of Gems $19.95, Mega-jug $79.95; includes heat-treating and faceting of your best gem. Bucket of garnet ore $4.95.

Other services available: Gift shop; snacks; gem cutting; restaurant opening in 2003.

Campground: Primitive sites $6.00.

Directions: Gem Mountain is located between Philipsburg and Hamilton on Montana Route 38 (Skalkaho road). 6 miles south of Philipsburg, turn from Highway 1 onto Highway 38 and drive 16 miles west, then follow the signs to the shop.

Digging for Sapphires

Digging:

Sapphires and gold can be found in low spots and up to 3 feet above bedrock. Dig the gravel near bedrock in an open pit. After loosening the gravel, screen the material in a shaker. Throw out the larger rocks, and sift out the sand. The remaining pea gravel will fill your 5-gallon buckets. Be sure to clean your bedrock with a whiskbroom and scoop. For this step, a small pry tool or screwdriver is useful for loosening the pockets of gravel lodged in the bedrock. Sapphires and gold can rarely be seen until the gravel is washed and concentrated.

Concentrating:

Once your buckets are filled, the screened gravel can then be concentrated in a riffled jig. The jig separates the heavier gravel. Or you may hand-wash your gravel. The hand method is time-consuming, however, and can take you up to an hour per bucket. The riffled jig will reduce your buckets of gravel down to ½ bucket of heavy concentrates in as little as 30 minutes.

Further concentrate your gravel with a hand screen. Sapphires are heavier than the surrounding material, so when you bounce or shake the screen in a tub of water, they will cluster on the bottom center of the screen. A piece of wood is then held over the top of the screenbox, and the screenbox is flipped upside down so that the gravel falls on the board without getting mixed up. If this is done properly, the sapphires will be concentrated in the center of the gravel on the board. You then pick your sapphires out of the gravel with tweezers.

You can find sapphires in every color. The natural sapphire crystal structure is hexagonal, with triangle terminations that are often flat. The most commonly found color is green-blue. Blue sapphire is the best known color. Ruby is a red sapphire and is one of the most prized.

SECTION 2: Museums and Mine Tours

BUTTE

Mine Tour

Anselmo Mine Yard
Butte, MT 59701
Phone: (406) 723-3177; (800) 735-6814
www.butteinfo.org

Open: Mid-June–Labor Day 10:00 A.M.–
6:00 P.M. Monday–Friday.

Info: The Anselmo Mine Yard and headframe are located in the Butte Historic
District and constitute the best surviving
example of the surface support facilities
that once served the Butte mines during
Butte's heyday as a first-class mining district. The visitor can tour the site and
learn the history of mining in Butte.
Note: There are no rest rooms at this
location.

Admission: Free.

Directions: The mine yard is located at
the intersection of Caledonia and Excel-
sior Streets.

BUTTE

Mine View

The Berkeley Pit
Butte, MT 59701
Phone: (406) 723-3177; (800) 735-6814

Open: Daily March–November, morning–dusk.

Info: The Berkeley Pit was an open-pit
copper mine that started in 1955 and
closed in 1982. Almost $1\frac{1}{2}$ trillion tons of
material were removed from this pit. Two
communities and much of Butte's East
Side were purchased and torn down to
make way for this pit, which is 7,000 feet
long, 5,600 feet wide, and 1,600 feet deep.

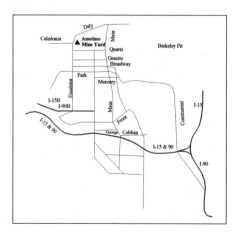

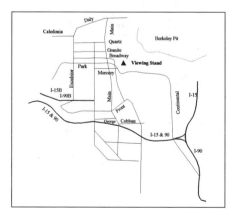

An observation stand can be reached by traveling Continental Drive. Coin-operated telescopes are available for close-up views. The gift shop adjacent to the stand is open in the summer and has souvenirs and information on the mine.

Admission: Free.

Other services available: Gift shop.

Directions: Off Continental Drive in Butte.

BUTTE

Museum 🏛

Butte-Silver Bow Visitor and
Transportation Center
1000 George Street
Butte, MT 59701
Phone: (406) 723-3177;
(800) 735-6814, ext. 98
Fax: (406) 723-1215

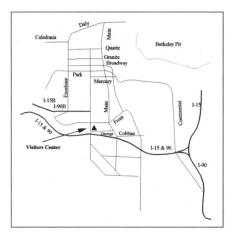

www.butteinfo.org

Open: Daily, May–Labor Day 8:00 A.M.–8:00 P.M., Labor Day–September 30 8:00 A.M.–5:00 P.M., October–May weekdays 9:00 A.M.–5:00 P.M.

Info: Displays present information about the geology and early settlement, the gold and silver area of Butte, the development of the "richest hill on earth," and the mining and smelting industry.

Admission: Free.

Directions: Just off I-15/I-90 at exit 126.

BUTTE

Museum 🏛

Mineral Museum
Montana College of Mineral Science and Technology
Butte, MT 59701
Phone: (406) 496-4414

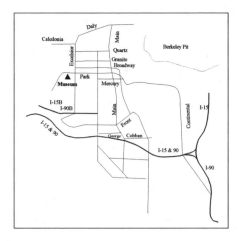

Open: Memorial Day–Labor Day, daily 9:00 A.M.–6:00 P.M.; May, September, and October 9:00 A.M.–4:00 P.M. Monday–Friday, 1:00–5:00 P.M. Saturday–Sunday. Guided tours can be arranged by calling.

Info: At present 1,300 of the 15,000 specimens in the museum's collection are on display. Displays include: the Highland Centennial Gold Nugget, weighing 27.475 troy ounces and found during placer mining in the Highland Mountains south of Butte; a systematic collection, after the Hey system, based on chemical composition; a variety of fluorescent minerals; an exhibit of minerals from Butte; and a display of minerals from Montana.

Admission: Free.

Directions: The Montana Tech campus is on Park Street, which can be reached from I-15/I-90 by taking the Mountain Street exit and traveling north to Park Street.

BUTTE

Museum 🏛

World Museum of Mining and 1899 Mining Camp
Butte, MT 59701
Phone: (406) 723-7211

Open: Daily, April 1–October 31, 9:00 A.M.–6:00 P.M.

Info: The World Museum of Mining and 1899 Mining Camp consists of a mining village with over three dozen structures located around the base of a real mining headframe. The museum sits on 12 acres of land surrounding the Orphan Girl mine, which once produced silver and zinc. Visitors can walk along the brick streets of the mining camp or start their tour in the hoist house. The hoist house has mining memorabilia and historic photos and also contains the museum gift shop. A recent addition to the village is a walk-through display on mining.

Admission: $4.00, under 12 free.

Other services available: Gift shop.

Directions: The museum is located west of Montana Tech. The campus is on Park Street, which can be reached from I-15/I-90 by taking the Mountain Street exit, and traveling north to Park Street. Go up the hill to the campus and past the Marcus Daly statue. Just beyond the statue, a sign in the middle of the street points straight ahead toward the museum. Watch for the Orphan Girl mine headframe, and turn left into the museum.

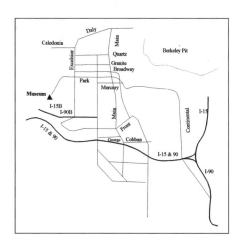

> ## Note:
>
> For the more adventurous or advanced rockhound, the Lewistown Area Chamber of Commerce has printed materials on some rockhounding spots on Bureau of Land Management (BLM) land.

EKALAKA

Museum 🏛

Carter County Museum
306 North Main Street
Ekalaka, MT 59324-0445
Phone: (406) 775-6886

Open: Daily, 9:00 A.M.–5:00 P.M. (closed noon–1:00 P.M.) Tuesday–Friday; 1:00–5:00 P.M. Saturday and Sunday.

Info: The Geological Department includes a fluorescent mineral display.

Admission: Free.

Other services available: Museum store.

Directions: Ekalaka is located at the junction of Montana Highway 7 and Carter County Road 325, 35 miles south of Baker, MT.

LEWISTOWN

Museum 🏛

Central Montana Museum
Lewistown Area Chamber of Commerce
P.O. Box 818, 408 Northeast Main
Lewistown, MT 59457
Phone: (406) 538-5436

Open: All year, 10:00 A.M.–4:00 P.M., 7 days/week.

Info: The Central Montana Museum attractions include four cases that display rocks and minerals and Yogo sapphires.

Admission: Donations appreciated.

Directions: Call for directions.

SECTION 3: Special Events and Tourist Information

TOURIST INFORMATION

State Tourist Agency

Travel Montana
301 South Park
P.O. Box 200533
Helena, MT 59620-0533
Phone: (406) 841-2870; (800) VISIT MT
www.visitmt.com

State Tourist Agency

Butte Chamber, Visitor, and
Transportation Center
1000 George Street
Butte, MT 59701
www.butteinfo.org

NEBRASKA

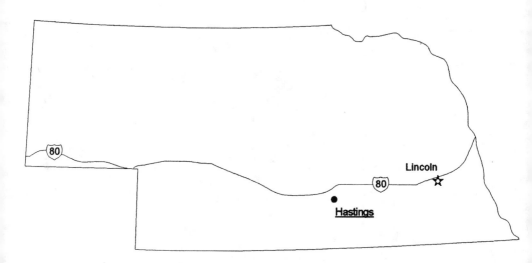

State Gemstone: Blue Agate
State Stone/Rock: Prairie Agate (1967)

SECTION 1: **Fee Dig Sites and Guide Services**

No information available.

SECTION 2: **Museums and Mine Tours**

HASTINGS

Museum

Hastings Museum of Natural and
Cultural History
1330 North Burlington Avenue
P.O. Box 1286
Hastings, NE 68902-1286
Phone: (402) 461-2399; (800) 508-4629
Fax: (402) 461-2379
E-mail: museum@alltel.net
www.hastingsmuseum.org

Open: Monday–Saturday 9:00 A.M.–
8:00 P.M., Sunday 10:00 A.M.–6:00 P.M.
Closed Thanksgiving and Christmas Day.

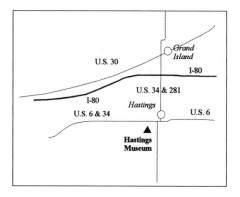

Info: The museum has numerous specimens of minerals and rocks on display. The museum also features a fluorescent mineral display, as well as a display of translucent slabs.
Admission: Adults $5.00, seniors $4.50, children $3.00.
Other services available: Lied Super Screen Theater, planetarium.
Directions: Located at 14th and Burlington (State Highway 281) in Hastings.

LINCOLN

Museum

University of Nebraska State Museum
307 Morrill Hall
Lincoln, NE 68588-0338
Phone: (402) 472-2642
E-mail: elephant@unl.edu
www.museum.unl.edu

Open: Monday–Saturday 9:30 A.M.–
4:30 P.M., Sundays and most holidays
1:30–4:30 P.M., closed on major holidays.

Info: This is the largest natural history museum in Nebraska; it has numerous specimens of minerals and rocks on display. The museum also has a fluorescent mineral display.

Admission: Adults $4.00, children 5–18 $2.00.

Directions: Exit I-80 at 27th Street and follow signs to Vine Street, then turn right. An alternate route is to take I-180 to the 14th Street exit and follow signs to the State Fair Park entrance. Go past the State Fair Park entrance to Vine Street, then turn right. Vine Street leads to 14th Street. Turn left to Morrill Hall. Limited parking during weekdays is available in front of the Hall; on week-

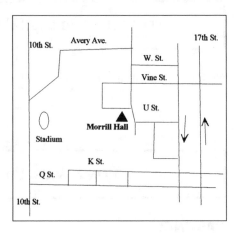

ends, additional parking is available in Lot 17c. Public parking is available within 10 minutes' walking distance from the hall.

SECTION 3: Special Events and Tourist Information

TOURIST INFORMATION

State Tourist Agency

Nebraska Division of Travel & Tourism
Department of Economic Development
Box 98907
Lincoln, NE 68509-8907
Phone: (877) NEBRASKA
www.visitnebraska.org

NORTH DAKOTA

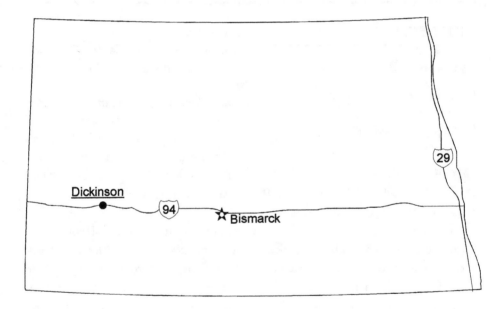

No information available.

DICKINSON

Museum

Dakota Dinosaur Museum
200 Museum Drive
Dickinson, ND 58601
Phone: (701) 225-3466
www.dakotadino.com

Open: Memorial Day–Labor Day 9:00 A.M.–6:00 P.M. Check with museum for winter hours.

Info: The museum has exhibits of rocks and minerals. New exhibits include borax from California, turquoise from Arizona, and fluorescent minerals. Also on display are "aurora crystals," natural quartz crystals from Arkansas, which have been subjected to a process of plasma ionization that deposits atomically thin layers of titanium, which then interacts with the crystal structure.

Admission: Adults $6.00, children 4–12

$3.00. Call for group rates.

Other services available: Gift shop with rock and mineral specimens.

Other local attractions in the Museum Center at Dickinson include:

▪ Joachim Regional Museum (open all year): Local artifacts and displays

▪ Pioneer Machinery Museum (10:00 A.M.–4:00 P.M. Memorial Day–Labor Day)

▪ Prairie Outpost Park (10:00–11:00 A.M. and 1:00–3:00 P.M. Memorial Day–Labor Day): Historical buildings include house, general store, post office, Burlington Northern depot, church, rural school, pioneer stone house, chapel, Scandinavian stabbur, and coal mine entrance.

Directions: From I-94 take exit 61 (Route 22). Take Route 22 south to the first traffic light, and turn left on Museum Drive.

SECTION 3: Special Events and Tourist Information

TOURIST INFORMATION

State Tourist Agency

North Dakota Tourism Department
Bismark, ND 58501
Phone: (701) 328-2525;
(800) HELLO-ND (435-5663)
www.ndtourism.com

OREGON

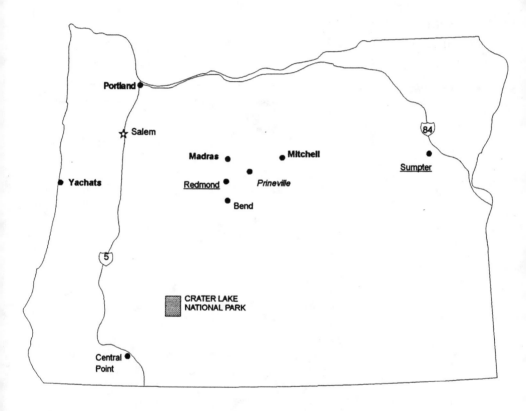

State Gemstone: Sunstone (1987)
State Stone/Rock: Thunderegg (1965)

Rockhounding in Oregon

From the early days of the lapidary hobby in America, Oregon has played a major role. Many of Oregon's treasures are in the quartz family: thundereggs or geodes (agate or jasper), agate, picture jasper, agatized wood, and carnelian. In the state one may also find gold, obsidian, cinnabar, zeolite, and more. Not all are found at fee dig sites; at the fee dig sites listed here, one may find thundereggs, moss agate, picture jasper, ledge agate, and petrified cypress. For the more adventurous, the Chambers of Commerce in Madras and Prineville have helpful information on prospecting areas.

Oregon Thundereggs

The Oregon state rock is the thunderegg. Thundereggs are usually found in volcanic ash and could be up to 60 million years old. They were named by the Warm Spring Indians, whose legend goes as follows:

> Mt. Hood and Mt. Jefferson, two adjacent snow-capped peaks that tower over central Oregon, would at times become angry with each other. They would rob the nests of the thunderbirds and hurl the eggs at each other.

In reality, the round shape of the thundereggs is due to the fact that the agates were formed in pockets created by steam and gases in hardening volcanic flows. When sliced and polished, the interiors can contain many colors of silica materials or crystals. They are used to make jewelry and rock products. The most beautiful are found in central Oregon. The town of Prineville claims to be the "agate capital of the U.S." There are also several areas in eastern Oregon that produce specimens.

Thunderegg

MADRAS / *Native • Easy to Difficult*

Dig for Thundereggs *T*

The following gems or minerals may be found:

• Thundereggs, agate (ledge agate material), moss agate, jasper, polka-dot jasp-agate, rainbow agate

Richardson's Recreational Ranch
Gateway Route, Box 440
Madras, OR 97741
Phone: (541) 475-2680; (541) 475-2839; (800) 433-2680

Open: Digging all year, weather permitting, all day. Office hours: 7:00 A.M.–5:00 P.M., 7 days/week.

Info: Digging for thundereggs requires rock picks, which are available for free day use. Digging for ledge agate requires chisels, wedges, and hard rock mining tools. Tools are available for sale at the shop, or bring your own. All diggings are easily accessible by road. Material is also available at the office.

Richardson's Recreational Ranch is a family-owned and -operated enterprise providing year-round family recreation. It is also a working cattle ranch.

Rates: Call for fees.

Other services available: Rock shop: Buy thundereggs, moss agate, jasper, jasp-agate, Oregon sunstone, rainbow agate, and other gems and minerals. Purchase rough or finished products. Also on sale are Richardson's high-speed sanders and sphere machines, and other brands of lapidary machines and supplies.

Free campground area for rockhounds; no hookups. Free showers at shop for customers.

Directions: Drive 11 miles north of Madras on U.S. 97. Then turn right, and drive 3 miles to the ranch office.

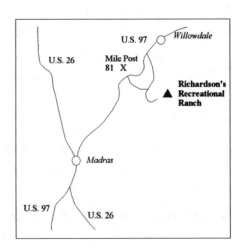

MITCHELL / *Native ▪ Easy to Moderate*

Dig for Thundereggs *T*

The following gems or minerals may be found:

▪ **Thundereggs**

Lucky Strike Geodes
Leonard "Kop" Kopcinski
P.O. Box 128
Mitchell, OR 97750
Phone: (541) 462-3073
E-mail: info@luckystrikemine.com
www.luckystrikemine.com

Open: Mid-May–November (weather permitting) 8:00 A.M.– 5:00 P.M. Closed Tuesday and Wednesday.

Info: Dig your own, or select from pre-dug material. Kop also owns another mine, the Valley View, which he may take you to upon request (weather permitting). If the weather is bad or if late snow has the mines closed, Kop has 50 tons of thundereggs in Mitchell that you can pick through. Digging for thundereggs requires rock picks which you should supply if

possible. Limited assistance is available.

Rates: You dig: $1.00/pound.

Other services available: Rock shop: Buy thundereggs, moss agate, and picture jasper. Purchase rough or finished products. The shop displays a large collection of picture jasper and other gems polished or made into jewelry (not for sale).

Free primitive campground; no hookups. Spring water is available.

Directions: The Lucky Strike mine is located in Crook County. From Prineville, drive east on U.S. 26 for 33 miles to a point between mileposts 49 and 50. Cross the cattle guard on the left then travel 0.8 miles on Forest Road 27 to the intersection with Forest Road 2730, then 11.2 miles on Forest Road 2730 to Forest Road 200. Follow the signs on Forest Road 200 another 2 miles to the mine. The Valley View is another 2 miles up the road.

YACHATS / *Native*

Find Your Own *T*

The following gems or minerals may be found:

▪ **Agates, jasper**

City of Yachats Visitors Center and Chamber of Commerce
P.O. Box 728
Yachats, OR 97498
Phone: (541) 547-3530; (800) 929-0477

Info: Stroll the beaches and collect agates and jasper. The most plentiful agate and jasper deposits are present on beaches

Authors' Note

Our first experience with thundereggs was at the Lucky Strike Mine owned and run by Leonard "Kop" Kopcinski. At 84, Kop is a rugged individualist, who will share with you his ideas on subjects dear to the hearts of many Westerners: private property; mining claims, and the individual's rights to them. The Lucky Strike is located in the Ochaco National Forest; the nearest town is Mitchell, Oregon. The drive up the mountain is breathtaking, and once you are at the mine, the scenery is tranquil. We parked our RV at the mine and woke up to chipmunks searching for handouts, and deer walking the path to the thunderegg mine.

Walt, Kop's sidekick, took us up to the dig in a pickup and showed us how to pull the thundereggs out of the ground with picks. They were plentiful.

Back at the mine office, Kop proceeded to show us tips on identifying good thundereggs. We shipped a hundred pounds of the beauties home (the packaging store sure appreciated our business).

Kop has a collection of some of the finest picture jasper in the world. He also has polished and unpolished pieces of picture jasper and thunderegg slabs for sale. We picked out some that had definite landscaped appearances: mountains, clouds, sunsets, and one the kids said looked like Darth Vader.

Kop plans to build a mineral museum on his property in Mitchell to display the extensive collection of minerals he has accumulated over the years.

Cutting Thundereggs

After shipping the thundereggs home, the authors decided that they "had to have" a means to find out what was inside them. They visited their local rock shop and were able to purchase a 10" diamond saw and an arbor (used for rock polishing). This used equipment had been customized by a lapidarist and had built-in shelves and electrical connections—a real find.

backed by sandstone bluffs and along the shoreline, where you can see patches of gravel. The best beaches are those that have exposed basalt near them where the sea can pound on the rock to release the embedded beauties. Another good place to look is along the shore of any rocky stream or river where it crosses a beach. Often agate washed out of basalt high in the Coast Range will be carried on water-courses down to the sea. Some agate beds are uncovered year round, while others are only open at unpredictable intervals. The most successful hunter is one who haunts the beaches on the out-running tides from December through March. Stonefield Beach Wayside, 6 miles south of Yachats, is one of the best beaches for all kinds of beachcombing. **Admission:** Free.

SECTION 2: Museums and Mine Tours

CENTRAL POINT

Museum

Crater Rock Museum
Roxy Ann Gem and Mineral Society, Inc.
P.O. Box 3999, 2002 Scenic Avenue
Central Point, OR 97502
Phone: (541) 664-6081

Open: Tuesday, Thursday, and Saturday, 10:00 A.M.–4:00 P.M.
Info: Founded in 1954, the museum contains excellent specimens of minerals, thundereggs, fossils, geodes, and cut and polished gemstones. The collection of minerals is arranged in a sequence useful for understanding minerals, how they are used, and their content.

A large meteorite, amber displays, and an excellent display of cut and pol-ished sections of petrified wood, identified as to species, are on display.

The museum is owned by the Roxy Ann Gem and Mineral Society, Inc., a nonprofit organization. Programs for school students, including classroom displays, are available. The society also offers: access to the earth science library, field trips to collecting sites, and workshops on lapidary arts, faceting, jewelry design, and fabrication.
Admission: Free.
Directions: Traveling south on I-5, take Exit 35 and follow Highway 99 to Scenic Avenue. There is a highway sign for the museum. Scenic Avenue is marked by an overhead yellow caution light; turn left onto Scenic Avenue to the museum.

Traveling north on I-5, take Exit 32,

> **Agate** results from silica filling empty gas pockets or cracks in rock, creating nodules or seams of agate. Since only limited amounts of foreign minerals are included, the resulting agate is generally pure. It ranges from clear to translucent when held up to the light. Clear agate with no color or pattern is called white agate; orangish-red agate is carnelian. Sard is clear to translucent agate with a yellow-orange to dark brown tinting.
>
> **Jasper** is an opaque stone, a variety of chert, resulting from deposits within sedimentary material. It contains a high percentage of impurities, which gives it high coloration.

turn left, and follow Pine Street through Central Point to the stoplights for Highway 99. Turn right on Highway 99 and travel for 2 miles. There is a highway sign for the museum. Scenic Avenue is marked by an overhead yellow caution light; turn left onto Scenic Avenue to the museum.

REDMOND

Point of Interest

Petersen's Rock Garden
7930 S.W. 77th Street
Redmond, OR 97756
Phone: (541) 382-5574

Open: All year. Summer hours: 9:00 A.M.–6:00 P.M. museum, 9:00 A.M.–9:00 P.M. outside. Winter hours: 9:00 A.M.–4:30 P.M. museum, 9:00 A.M.–dusk outside.

Info: This unusual garden is the 17-year creation of Rasmur Petersen, a Danish immigrant farmer, and has 4 acres of miniature rock structures. Almost all the rocks used come from within an 85-mile radius of the gardens. Included are petrified wood, agate, jasper, thundereggs, malachite, lava, and obsidian.

The museum houses thousands of rock specimens and a fine fluorescent rock display.

Admission: Donation requested; adults $3.00, children 12–16 $1.50, children 6–11 $0.50.

Other services: Gift shops; picnic area with tables, fireplaces, and free-roaming peacocks, ducks, and chickens to help you with your lunch.

Directions: 2½ miles west of Highway 97 between Redmond and Bend.

SUMPTER

Mining Dredge Tour

Sumpter Valley Dredge State Heritage Area
Greater Sumpter Chamber of Commerce
P.O. Box 250
Sumpter, OR 97877
Phone: (541) 894-2486; (800) 551-6949
Fax: (541) 894-2445
www.triax.com/sumpter

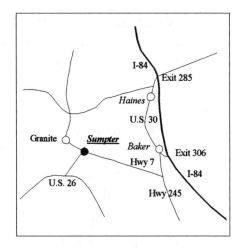

Hours: 10:00 A.M.–4:00 P.M.

Info: View a gold dredge: the dredge that rests at the edge of Sumpter was built by the Sumpter Valley Dredge Co. in 1935. It shut down between 1942 and 1945 because of World War II, then operated under various owners until all dredging in the valley ceased in 1954. The dredge recovered more than $4.5 million during its heyday, and over $10 million in gold was recovered by dredging in Sumpter Valley alone.

Admission: Free.

Other attractions: Tour the historic gold rush towns of Sumpter and Granite.

Directions: Take Exit 306 on I-84, then follow State Highway 7 west to Sumpter. Off OR 7, 30 miles west of Baker City.

PRINEVILLE

Crook County Chamber of Commerce

390 N. Fairview
Prineville, OR 97754
Phone: (541) 447-6304
Fax: (541) 447-6537

Info: Crook County, Oregon claims the title "Rockhound Capital of the World." The Chamber of Commerce provides a helpful guide to types of rocks you can expect to find in the area. Call for cost.

The Chamber of Commerce also sponsors a Rockhounds Pow-Wow in mid-June each year. Amateur rockhounds and commercial dealers bring equipment and materials to sell or trade.

ANNUAL EVENT

Bohemia Mining Days

Bohemia Mining Days
Cottage Grove, OR 97424
Phone: (541) 942-2411
E-mail: cgchamber@oip.net
www.bohemiaminingdays.org

Info: Third week in July; features Oregon State Gold Panning Championship, Western States Gold Mining Exposition, treasure hunt, concerts, demonstrations.

TOURIST INFORMATION

State Tourist Agency

Oregon Tourism Commission
775 Summer Street NE
Salem, OR 97301
Phone: (503) 986-0000; (800) 547-7842
Fax: (503) 986-0001
www.traveloregon.com

SOUTH DAKOTA

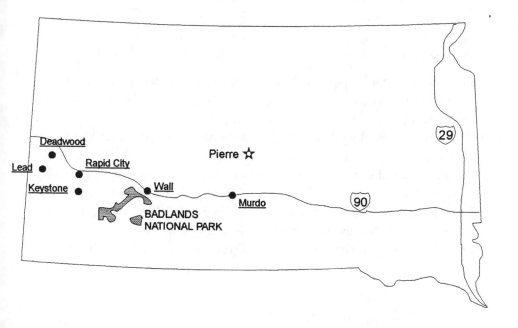

State Gemstone: Fairburn Agate (1966)
State Mineral/Stone: Rose Quartz (1966)

DEADWOOD / *Easy*

Pan for Gold *T*

The following gems or minerals may be found:

- Gold

Broken Boot Gold Mine
735 Main Street
Deadwood, SD 57732
Phone: (605) 578-9997

Open: Mid-May–mid-September, 8:30 A.M.–5:30 P.M., 7 days/week.
Panning fee: $4.75.
Other services available: Restrooms.
Info: For more information on the mine tour and the City of Deadwood, see listing in Section 2.
Directions: Located at the south end of Historic Deadwood, at the junction of Upper Main Street and Highway 14A.

KEYSTONE / *Easy*

Pan for Gold *T*

The following gems or minerals may be found:

- Gold

Big Thunder Gold Mine
Box 459
Keystone, SD 57751
Phone: (605) 666-4847; (800) 314-3917

Open: June–Labor Day 8:00 A.M.–8:00 P.M.; May, September–October 9:00 A.M.–6:00 P.M. 7 days/week.
Admission for panning: $3.95 with mine tour.
Info: The mine is handicapped accessible.
Other services available: Restrooms. For more information on the mine tour, see listing in Section 2.
Directions: Off Highway 40.

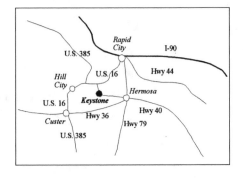

LEAD / *Easy*

Pan for Gold *T*

The following gems or minerals may be found:

- **Gold**

Black Hills Mining Museum
323 West Main Street
P.O. Box 694
Lead, SD 57754
Phone: (605) 584-1605
E-mail: bhminmus@mato.com
www.mining-museum.blackhills.com

Open: All year. May–August 9:00 A.M.–5:00 P.M.; September–May, Tuesday–Saturday 9:00 A.M.–4:30 P.M. Off-season tours: 9:45 A.M., 11:00 A.M., 12:30 P.M., 2:00 P.M., 3:30 P.M.

Cost for panning: $4.25–$5.00 in addition to museum admission.

Info: For more information on the museum, see listing in Section 2.

Other services: Simulated mine tour (see Section 2 for more information); gift shop, which sells gold panning supplies.

Directions: Lead is located on U.S. 85, south of I-90.

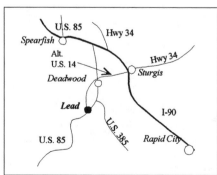

WALL / *Native • Difficult*

Hunt for Rocks and Minerals *T*

The following gems or minerals may be found:

- **Agates**

Buffalo Gap National Grassland
Wall Ranger District
Box 425
Wall, SD 57790
Phone: (605) 279-2125

Open: Visitor Center open all year, Memorial Day–Labor Day 8:00 A.M.–6:00 P.M.; rest of the year 8:00 A.M.–4:30 P.M., Monday–Friday.

Info: The surface collection of rocks and minerals for personal use is allowed without a permit. The collection of these items for future barter, sale, etc., would require a permit, as would any excavation or surface disturbance.

The Buffalo Gap National Grassland map is available for $4.00. This map shows the different land status of public and private lands. To request a map, call (605) 279-2125. Cost is $6.42 and checks should be made out to: BNHA, National Forest Service. The map can also be purchased at the visitor center in Wall.

Admission: Free.

Directions: Take exit 110 off I-90, travel north to South Boulevard. Turn left on South Boulevard for two blocks, then turn right on Main Street to the visitor center.

DEADWOOD

Mine tour 🏛

Broken Boot Gold Mine
735 Main Street
Deadwood, SD 57732
Phone: (605) 578-9997

Open: Mid-May–mid-September, 8:30 A.M.–6:30 P.M., 7 days/week.
Info: Step back in time to experience late 1800s gold mining. Visitors receive a souvenir share of stock in the Broken Boot Mine after the tour.

The City of Deadwood is a designated National Historic Landmark, and there are many recreation activities nearby.
Admission: Adults: $4.75, students 13–18 $2.50, children 1–12 $1.00.
Other services available: Mine tour, gift shop, restrooms.
Directions: Located at the south end of Historic Deadwood, at the junction of Upper Main Street and Highway 14A.

KEYSTONE

Mine tour 🏛

Big Thunder Gold Mine
Box 459
Keystone, SD 57751
Phone: (605) 666-4847; (800) 314-3917
www.bigthundergoldmine.com

Open: June–Labor Day 8:00 A.M.–8:00 P.M., May and September–October 9:00 A.M.–6:00 P.M., 7 days/week.
Info: Relive the experience of 1880s gold mining. Free samples of gold ore are given on the underground mine tour. The mine is handicapped accessible.
Admission: Adults $7.40, children 6–12 $4.40.
Other services available: Mine tour; gift shop; restrooms.
Directions: Off Highway 40.

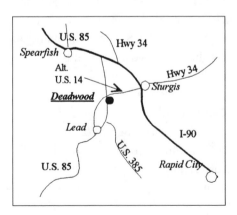

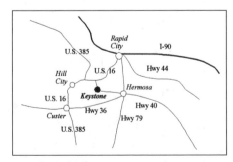

LEAD

Museum

Black Hills Mining Museum
323 West Main Street
P.O. Box 694
Lead, SD 57754
Phone: (605) 584-1605
E-mail: bhminmus@mato.com
www.mining-museum.blackhills.com

Open: All year. May–August 9:00 A.M.–5:00 P.M. daily; September–May 9:00 A.M.–4:30 P.M. Tuesday–Saturday.

Info: The Black Hills Mining Museum is dedicated to the preservation of the rich mining heritage of the Black Hills of South Dakota. The museum offers tours of a simulated underground mine, exhibits, displays, photos, and artifacts to explain the mining process. Gold panning is offered at an additional cost. The underground mine is a re-creation of an underground level of the Homestake Mine, complete with over 20 full-size displays. During the tour you will explore a stope; witness a simulated blast; and see an underground cage station, powder and cap magazines, mine locomotives and ore cars, and much more. The museum also offers video presentations on changes in mining techniques over the past century.

Admission: Adults $4.50, seniors (60+) $4.00, children (7–college) $3.50; family rate $15.00. Children under 6 free.

Directions: Lead is located on U.S. 85, south of I-90.

LEAD

Museum

Homestake Visitor Center
160 West Main Street
Lead, SD 57754-0887
Phone: (605) 584-3110; (888) 701-0164
www.homestaketour.com

Open: September–May, 8:00 A.M.–5:00 P.M., Monday–Friday. June–August, 8:00 A.M.–5:00 P.M., Monday–Friday, 10:00 A.M.–5:00 P.M. Saturday and Sunday. Tours available 8:30 A.M.–4:30 P.M., every half hour, May–September only.

Info: Homestake is more than a museum; it is the world's oldest continuously operated gold mine. A tour of the Homestake offers the opportunity to witness the changes in American gold mining from the early days of panning to current high-tech mining. Through displays and mining artifacts, you will learn about mining and ore processing as well as about the mine,

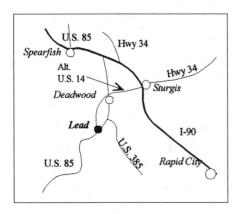

which extends more than 8,000 feet below the town of Lead. On completion of the tour you will receive a sample of ore that was drilled from the mine.

Admission: Adults $5.25, seniors $4.75, students (6–18) $4.25, children 5 and under free. Family rate $15.00.

Other services available: Gift shop.

Directions: The visitor center is located on the edge of the open cut.

MURDO

Museum 🏛

National Rockhound and Lapidary
Hall of Fame
South Dakota Pioneer Museum
HC 74, Box 21
Murdo, SD 57559-9215
Phone: (605) 669-2691
Fax: (605) 669-3217

Open: Memorial Day–Labor Day 8:00 A.M.–9:00 P.M.; fall and winter hours vary.

Info: The National Rockhound Hall of Fame was dedicated on June 15, 1987. The hall recognizes rockhounds and lapidaries, both living and dead, who have had great influence on the hobby. The Zeitner Gem, Mineral, and Fossil Collection, an extensive collection, is on display at the hall. There is a good variety of minerals, including one 8-foot display of minerals collected in South Dakota. The lapidary cases have a mixture of interesting materials, such as agates from most of the U.S. states, Mexico, and Australia. There are also

examples of different lapidary techniques, including pictures, cabochons, sculptures, a fluorescent case, and a case of spheres.

Admission: Adults $7.50, children (6–13) $4.00, children (under 6) free.

Other services available: The hall is part of the Pioneer Auto and Antique Town (25 buildings).

Directions: Exit 192 on I-90, in Murdo.

RAPID CITY

Museum 🏛

South Dakota School of Mines and Technology
Museum of Geology
501 East St. Joseph Street
Rapid City, SD 57701
Phone: (605) 394-2467;
(800) 554-8162, ext. 2467
www.sdsmt.edu/services/museum

Open: All year; closed holidays. Memorial Day–Labor Day, Monday–Saturday 8:00 A.M.–6:00 P.M. Sunday 12:00–6:00 P.M. Rest of the year, Monday–Friday 8:00 A.M.–5:00 P.M., Saturday 9:00 A.M.–4:00 P.M., Sunday 1:00–4:00 P.M.

Info: Specializes in local specimens including minerals from the Black Hills, such as Fairborn agates, stibnite, and gypsum crystals.

Admission: Free.

Directions: Take West Boulevard south from I-90 to Main Street. Take Main Street east to the School of Mines.

SECTION 3: Special Events and Tourist Information

TOURIST INFORMATION

State Tourist Agency

South Dakota Department of Tourism
711 East Wells Avenue
Pierre, SD 57501-3369
Phone: (800) SDAKOTA (732-5682);
(800) 952-3625
E-mail: sdinfo@state.sd.us
www.travelsd.com

WASHINGTON

State Gemstone: Petrified Wood (1975)

SECTION 1: Fee Dig Sites and Guide Services

RAVENSDALE / *Native • Guide Services*

Find pyrite, quartz, and other gems and minerals *T*

The following gems or minerals may be found:

▪ Pyrite, quartz crystals, garnets, pink topaz, fluorite, barite, fluorescent minerals, amber, plant fossils*, and fossil clams*

Bob Jackson's Geology Adventures
P.O. Box 809
Ravensdale, WA 98051
Phone/Fax: (425) 413-1122

E-mail: bob@geologyadventures.com
(*Note:* often in the field for weeks at a time so it may take a while to get a return e-mail.)
www.geologyadventures.com

Open: Between July and September; must be scheduled in advance.
Info: A variety of tours are available, including ones geared toward kids.
Rates: Call for rates.
Directions: Call for directions.

* See our upcoming sequel on fossils for more information on fossil collecting.

SECTION 2: Museums and Mine Tours

CASTLE ROCK

Museum

Mount St. Helens National Volcanic Monument
Monument Headquarters
42218 Northeast Yale Bridge Road
Amboy, WA 98601
Phone: (360) 247-3900
Fax: (360) 247-3901
www.fs.fed.us/gpnf/mshnvm

Open: All year, 8:00 A.M.–5:00 P.M. Monday–Friday.

Info: Other locations within the National Monument are not open all year. They are open on weekends as well as weekdays, and may have different hours than the headquarters.

Many of the gems and minerals discussed in this book were formed as a result of volcanic activity. At Mount St. Helens in Washington, visitors can witness the power of the volcano. On May 18, 1980, Mount St. Helens erupted explosively, after 120 years of quiet. When the eruption was over, the top

1,300 feet of the mountain was gone. Several visitor centers have been constructed, providing views and interpretations of the eruption, along with displays, some of which focus on geology.

Admission: Adults $3.00, children 5–15 $1.00, children 4 and under free (for one-day pass).

Directions: The National Monument, which is located near the Washington-Oregon border, can be reached from I-5. State Highways 503, 504, and 505, and U.S. 12, provide access to different areas.

ELLENSBURG

Museum

Kittitas County Historical Museum and Society
P.O. Box 265
114 East Third
Ellensburg, WA 98926-0265
Phone: (509) 925-3778

Open: All year, October–April 11:00 A.M.–3:00 P.M. May–September 10:00 A.M.–4:00 P.M., Tuesday–Saturday.

Info: The museum houses the vast collection of polished rock and petrified wood belonging to the Rollinger Brothers, who donated the collection to the citizens of Kittitas County.

Admission: Free; donations accepted.

Directions: Ellensburg is located at the intersection of I-90 and I-82. Call for directions to the library.

PULLMAN

Museum 🏛

Washington State University
Department of Geology
Physical Science Building
Pullman, WA 99164-2812
Phone: (509) 335-3009

Open: When school is in session. Academic year hours: Monday–Friday 8:00 A.M.–5:00 P.M. Summer hours: Monday–Friday 7:30 A.M.–4:00 P.M.

Group tours available on weekends by prior reservations.

Info: The Lyle and Lela Jacklin collection of silicified wood and minerals is on display in the Harold E. Culver Memorial Room (Room 124) in the Physical Science Building. The collection contains over 1,700 specimens collected from key sites in the western United States.

Admission: Free.

Directions: Call for directions to the university.

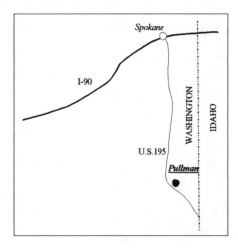

SEATTLE

Museum

Burke Museum of Natural History
University of Washington
Box 353010
Seattle, WA 98195-3010
Phone: (206) 543-5590
E-mail: receipt@uwashington.edu
www.burkemuseum.org

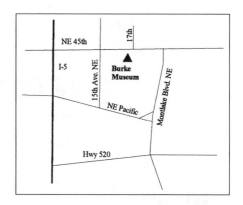

Open: Daily 10:00 A.M.–5:00 P.M.
Info: Exhibits present the historical geology of Washington, as well as a walk-through volcano, to give you the "inside" story. Also has rocks and minerals on display.

Admission: Adults $6.50, seniors $5.00, students $3.00, children under 6 free.
Directions: From I-5, take NE 45th Street exit east. Parking is available just south of the university campus.

SECTION 3: Special Events and Tourist Information

TOURIST INFORMATION

State Tourist Agency

Washington State Tourism
101 General Administration Building
P.O. Box 42500
Olympia, WA 98504-2500
Phone: (800) 544-1800; (360) 725-5052
E-mail: tourism@cted.wa.gov
www.experiencewashington.com

WYOMING

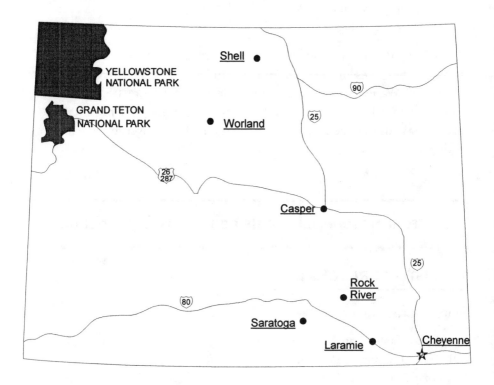

State Gemstone: Nephrite Jade (1967)

SECTION 1: Fee Dig Sites and Guide Services

SHELL / *Native • Easy to Difficult*

Dig for Moss Agate *T*

The following gems or minerals may be found:

- Dendritic agate

Trapper Galloway Ranch
Floyd "Kit" Smith
P.O. Box 95 .
Shell, WY 82441
Phone: (307) 765-2971

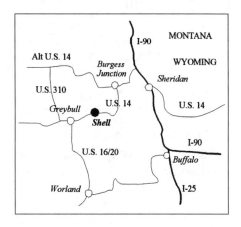

Open: Mine open after July 1, 7 days/week.

Info: The mine is up in the Bighorns at approximately 8,400 feet elevation. You can dig for agate at the mine, or a pile of mined material is kept at the ranch. This material can be picked through, and you can keep all that you find.

Fee for the mine: $150.00/day; keep all the material you want. Any material kept from the pile at the ranch will be charged $1.00/pound.

Directions: The ranch is located 1½ miles west of Shell.

SECTION 2: Museums and Mine Tours

CASPER

Museum 🏛

Tate Geological Museum
Casper College
125 College Drive
Casper, WY 82601
Phone: (307) 268-2447
E-mail: dbrown@caspercollege.edu
www.caspercollege.edu/tate/webpage.asp

Open: All year, 8:00 A.M.–6:00 P.M. Monday–Friday; 10:00 A.M.–3:00 P.M. weekends.

Info: The museum has exhibits of rocks and minerals, including a display of Wyoming jade and a display of fluorescent minerals.

Admission: Free.

Other services available: Gift shop.

Directions: Take Wolcott Avenue south from Yellowstone Highway (U.S. 20) to the Casper College Campus. Follow

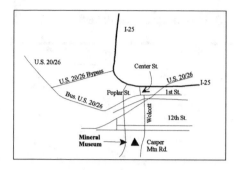

Wolcott to Casper Mountain Road (Highway 261) along campus; take the third left after College Drive, then first right to the Tate Museum.

CHEYENNE

Museum 🏛

Wyoming State Museum
2301 Central Avenue
Cheyenne, WY 82002
Phone: (307) 777-7022
Fax: (307) 777-5375
E-mail: wsm@state.wy.us
www.wyomuseumstate.wy.us

Open: May–October: Tuesday–Saturday 9:00 A.M.–4:30 P.M. November–April: Tuesday–Friday 9:00 A.M–4:30 P.M., Saturday 10:00 A.M.–2:00 P.M. Closed state and federal holidays.

Info: The Swamped With Coal gallery addresses trona, coal, the evolution of mining lamps, jade (nephrite), gold, diamonds, oil, natural gas, uranium, and bentonite. Special features include a swamp to coal mine model and an ore cart filled with examples of products visitors may have in their homes that are made with Wyoming raw materials; e.g., kitty litter is made from bentonite. The spin cubes are a hands-on activity which allows visitors to line up a mineral, the location it is found in the state, and what it is used to make.

Admission: Free.

Other services available: Museum store.

Directions: The museum is located on Central Avenue, one block south and east of the Wyoming State Capitol building.

LARAMIE

Museum 🏛

Geological Museum
University of Wyoming
P.O. Box 3006
Laramie, WY 82071-3006
Phone: (307) 766-4218
www.uwyo.edu/geomuseum

Open: All year, 8:00 A.M.–5:00 P.M., Monday–Friday. Weekends, 10:00 A.M.–3:00 P.M. Closed University holidays.

Info: The museum has exhibits of rocks and minerals, including a display of fluorescent minerals from Wyoming and from around the world.

Admission: Free.

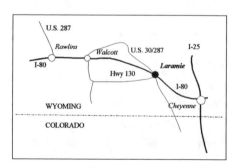

Directions: In the northwest corner of the university campus, next to the S.H. Knight Geology Building.

ROCK RIVER

Museum

Rock River Museum
North 2nd Street and Avenue C
Rock River, WY 82083
Phone: (307) 378-2386; (307) 378-2205

Open: Memorial Day–Labor Day or by appointment. Wednesday–Saturday 10:00 A.M.–3:00 P.M., Sunday noon–3:00 P.M.

Info: The museum has a display of fluorescent minerals and of rocks and minerals collected from the local area.

Admission: Free.

Directions: Rock River is located 39 miles north of Laramie on Highway 30/287.

SARATOGA

Museum

Saratoga Museum
104 Constitution Avenue
Saratoga, WY 82331
Phone: (307) 326-5511

Open: Memorial Day–Labor Day, 1:00–4:00 P.M.

Info: Minerals from around the world and educational displays of local geology.

Admission: Call for current rates.

Directions: Take the Route 130 exit off

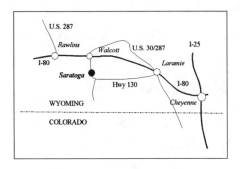

I-80 at Walcott, and drive south (or east) on 130 to Saratoga, or take Route 130 west (or north) from Laramie.

WORLAND

Museum

Washakie Museum
1115 Obie Sue
Worland, WY 82401
Phone: (307) 347-4102

Open: All year, 10:00 A.M.–5:00 P.M.

Info: Geology room contains assorted agates, crystals, a rock cycle display, an earthquake display, and minerals.

Admission: Free.

Directions: Call for directions.

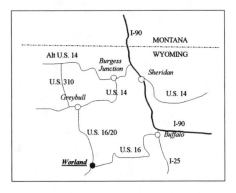

SECTION 3: Special Events and Tourist Information

ANNUAL EVENT

Symposium

A Symposium on Wyoming geology and a field trip is held each June. For more information:

Tate Geological Museum
Casper College
125 College Drive
Casper, WY 82601
Phone: (307) 268-2447

TOURIST INFORMATION

State Tourist Agency

Wyoming Business Council
Travel and Tourism
I-25 at College Drive
Cheyenne, WY 82002
Phone: (800) 225-5996; (307) 777-7777
Fax: (307) 777-2877
www.state.wy.us

Index by State

ALABAMA

Fee Dig Mines and Guide Services
　　　　None

Museums and Mine Tours
Anniston　　Anniston Museum of Natural History—gemstones, meteorite, artificial indoor cave

ALASKA

Fee Dig Mines and Guide Services
Fairbanks　　El Dorado Gold Mine—gold panning
　　　　Gold Dredge No. 8—gold panning
　　　　Chena Hot Springs Resort—gold panning

Museums and Mine Tours
Anchorage　　Stewart's Photo Shop—gem and mineral displays
Fairbanks　　El Dorado Gold Mine—working gold mine tour
　　　　Gold Dredge No. 8—gold dredge tour
　　　　University of Alaska Museum—minerals and gems from Alaska, Arctic Canada, and the Pacific Rim; includes gold and meteorites

ARIZONA

Fee Dig Mines and Guide Services
Apache Junction　　Apache Trails Tours—gold panning
Goldfield　　Goldfield Ghost Town, Scenic Railroad, and Mine Tours—gold panning

Museums and Mine Tours
Bisbee　　Queen Mine Tour—Tour a copper mine
Flagstaff　　Meteor Crater Enterprises, Inc.—View a meteor crater, museum of astrogeology

Goldfield	Goldfield Ghost Town, Scenic Railroad, and Mine Tours—Gold mine tour, museum, ghost town
	Superstition Mountain Museum—Geology, minerals, and mining
Phoenix	Arizona Mining and Mineral Museum—3,000 minerals on exhibit, minerals from AZ copper mines, piece of meteor crater meteorite, rocks from original moon landing, spheres, fluorescent mineral display
Sun City	The Mineral Museum—3,000 rocks and minerals from the U.S. and the world, with emphasis on minerals from AZ; Over 150 fluorescent rocks and minerals, most from Franklin and Sterling Hill, NJ
Sahuarita	ASARCO Mineral Discovery Center—Geology, mining, minerals, and tour of open-pit mine
Tucson	Arizona-Sonora Desert Museum—Mineral collection from Sonoran desert region
	Mineral Museum, University of Arizona—2,100 of 15,000 minerals on display; AZ minerals, meteorites, fluorescents, borate minerals

Annual Events

Quartzite	Gem & Mineral Shows—mid-January–mid-February
Scottsdale	Minerals of Arizona—Symposium 1 day in March
Tucson	Gem & Mineral Shows—first 2 weeks in February

ARKANSAS

Fee Dig Mines and Guide Services

Hot Springs	Coleman's Crystal Mines—Dig for quartz crystals
Jessieville	Jim Coleman Crystal Mines—Dig for quartz crystals
Mt. Ida	Fiddler's Ridge Rock Shop and Crystal Mines—Dig for quartz crystals
	Leatherhead Quartz Mining—Dig for quartz crystals
	Robbin's Mining Company—Dig for quartz crystals
	Sonny Stanley's Crystal Mine—Dig for quartz crystals
	Starfire Mine—Dig for quartz crystals
	Sweet Surrender Crystal Mine—Dig for quartz crystals
	Wegner's Crystal Mine—Dig for quartz crystals
Murfreesboro	Crater of Diamonds State Park—Dig and screen for diamonds, amethyst, agates, barite, calcite, jasper, quartz, other gems
Paron	Willis Crystal Mine and Gift Shop—Dig for quartz crystals

Museums and Mine Tours

Fayetteville   The University Museum—Quartz and other AR minerals
Little Rock   Geology Learning Center—AR gems, minerals, fossil fuels
State University A.S.U. Museum—Minerals, many from AR

Annual Events

Mt. Ida   Quartz Crystal Festival and World Championship Dig—Second weekend in October

CALIFORNIA

Fee Dig Mines and Guide Services

Angels Camp   Jensen's Pick & Shovel Ranch—Guided prospecting for gold
Coloma   Marshall Gold Digging State Historic Park—Gold panning
Columbia   Hidden Treasures Gold Mine Tours—Gold panning
Jackson   Kennedy Gold Mine—Gold panning
Lakeport   Lake County Visitors Information Center—Search for Lake County "diamonds" or "moon tears"
Mariposa   Little Valley Inn—Gold panning
Nevada City   Malakoff Diggins State Historic Park—Gold panning
Palo Verde   Opal Hill Fire Agate Mine—Dig for fire agate, micromount crystals, apatite, barite, calcite, clinoptilolite, fluorite, gypsum (curved)
Pine Grove   Roaring Camp Mining Co.—Pan for gold, rockhounding
Placerville   Gold Bug Mine and Hangtown's Gold Bug Park—Gold panning

Museums and Mine Tours

Allegany   Underground Gold Miners Tours and Museum—Tour an active gold mine
Angels Camp   Angels Camp Museum—Rocks and minerals; gold stamping mill, mining equipment
Avalon   Catalina Island Museum Society Inc.—Exhibits on mining on Catalina Island
Boron   Borax Global Visitors Center—Story of borax
  Boron Twenty Mule Team Museum—History of area borate mining
Coloma   Marshall Gold Discovery State Historic Park—Gold mining exhibit/museum
Columbia   Hidden Treasure Gold Mine—Tour of active gold mine
Death Valley   Furnace Creek Borax Museum—Rocks and minerals, featuring borax minerals

El Cajon	Heritage of the Americas Museum—Rocks, minerals, and meteorites
Fallbrook	Fallbrook Gem & Mineral Museum—Gems and minerals
Grass Valley	Empire Mine State Historic Park—Hardrock gold mine
Independence	Eastern California Museum—Exhibit depicts local mining
Jackson	Amador County Museum—Collection of mineral spheres from CA, UT, NV
	Kennedy Gold Mine Tours—Surface tour of gold mine
Julian	Eagle and High Peak Gold Mine Tours—Hardrock gold mine tour
	Julian Pioneer Museum—Rock and mineral display, gold mining tools and equipment displays
Lakeport	Lake County Museum—Minerals and gems from Lake County, CA
Los Angeles	Natural History Museum of Los Angeles County—52,000 specimens; minerals of CA; native gold, gems, and minerals
Mariposa	California State Mining and Mineral Museum—Gold from CA, gems and minerals from around the world
Needles	Needles Regional Museum—Needles blue agate, Colorado River pebble terrace stones
Nevada City	Malakoff Diggins State Historic Park—History of hydraulic gold mining
Pacific Grove	Pacific Grove Museum of Natural History—Monterey County rocks, fluorescent minerals
Paso Robles	El Paso des Robles Area Pioneer Museum—Display of local minerals
Placerville	Gold Bug Mine and Hangtown's Gold Bug Park—Tour hardrock gold mine
Quincy	Plumas County Museum—Exhibits on silver and copper mining in Plumas County
Rancho Palo Verdes	Point Vicente Interpretive Center—Exhibits on area geology
Redlands	San Bernardino County Museum—45,000 rocks, minerals, and gems
Ridgecrest	Maturango Museum—Small but well-rounded regional gem and mineral collection
Riverside	Jurupa Mountains Cultural Center—Crestmore minerals display, minerals from around the world on display and for sale, family education programs
	Riverside Municipal Museum—Rocks, minerals, gems, and regional geology
	World Museum of Natural History—Fluorescent minerals, meteorites, tektites, over 1,300 mineral spheres
San Diego	San Diego Natural History Museum—26,000 mineral specimens, includes minerals found in San Diego County mines

Santa Barbara	Department of Geological Sciences, U.C.S.B.—Gem and mineral collection, minerals and their tectonic settings
Shoshone	Shoshone Museum—Rock collection reflecting the geology of the area
Sierra City	Kentucky Mine and Museum—Exhibits of local gold and mercury mining
Sonora	Tuolomne County Museum—Gold from local mines
Yermo	Calico Ghost Town—Explore a silver mine
Yreka	Siskiyou County Courthouse—Gold exhibit
Yucca Valley	Hi-Desert Nature Museum—Rock and mineral collection, includes fluorescent minerals

Annual Events

| Boron | Rock Bonanza—weekend before Easter |
| Coloma | Marshall Gold Discovery State Historic Park: Gold Rush Days—end of September–beginning of October |

COLORADO

Fee Dig Mines and Guide Services

Idaho Springs	Argo Gold Mill—Pan for gold and gemstones
	Phoenix Mine—Pan for gold
Lake George (Tarryall)	Topaz Mountain Gem Mine—Screen for topaz, phenakite crystals in topaz, goshenite, quartz, feldspar

Museums and Mine Tours

Denver	Denver Museum of Natural History—2,000 specimens, includes gold, topaz, aquamarine, amazonite, and other Colorado minerals
Georgetown	Lebanon Silver Mine—Tour a silver mine
Golden	Geology Museum, Colorado School of Mines—50,000 specimens, minerals from Colorado and from around the world, gemstones and precious metals, cave exhibit
Idaho Springs	Argo Gold Mill—Historic gold mill, mining museum, Double Eagle Gold Mine
	Edgar Experimental Mine—Tour an experimental mine (silver, gold, lead, copper)
	Phoenix Mine—See a working underground hardrock mine (gold, silver)
Leadville	Matchless Mine—Tour a gold mine
	National Mining Hall of Fame and Museum—Story of the American mining industry from coal to gold

Silverton   Mayflower Gold Mill—Tour a gold mill

Old Hundred Gold Mine Tour, Inc.—Gold mine tour

San Juan County Historical Museum—Minerals and gems from the Silverton area

CONNECTICUT

Fee Dig Mines and Guide Services

None

Museums and Mine Tours

East Granby   Old New-Gate Prison and Copper Mine—Tour an old copper mine

Greenwich   Bruce Museum of Arts and Science—Minerals and rocks

New Haven   Peabody Museum of Natural History—Minerals of New England and the world

DELAWARE

Fee Dig Mines and Guide Services

None

Museums and Mine Tours

Newark   Delaware Academy of Science, Iron Hill Museum—DE minerals, fluorescent minerals

University of Delaware, Mineralogical Museum—5,000 specimens (1,000 on display), crystals, gems, minerals

DISTRICT OF COLUMBIA

Fee Dig Mines and Guide Services

None

Museums and Mine Tours

Smithsonian Institution, National Museum of Natural History—Gems and minerals

FLORIDA

Fee Dig Mines and Guide Services

None

Museums and Mine Tours

Mulberry   Mulberry Phosphate Museum—Exhibits on the phosphate industry

Tampa   Ed and Bernadette Marcin Museum, University of Florida—Minerals and gemstones mainly from FL and the western U.S.

GEORGIA

Fee Dig Mines and Guide Services

Cleveland   Gold'n Gem Grubbin—Dig and pan for gold, sapphires, rubies, emeralds, amethyst, topaz

Dahlonega   Consolidated Gold Mine—Gold panning

Crisson Gold Mine—Pan gold sands or enriched gemstone ore

Helen   Gold Mine of Helen, GA—Pan gold sand or enriched gemstone ore

Lincolnton   Graves Mountain—Search for audite, lazulite, pyrophyllite, kyanite, hematite, pyrite, ilmenite, muscovite, fuchsite, barite, sulfur, blue quartz, quartz crystals, microcrystals such as woodhouseite, variscite, strengite, phosphosiderite, cacoxenite, crandallite

Museums and Mine Tours

Atlanta   Fernbank Museum of Natural History—Joachim gem collection containing 400 cut and polished gemstones

Fernbank Science Center—Gems, carved opals, meteorites

Cartersville   William Weinman Mineral Museum—2,000 specimens, gems and minerals from the state; simulated cave

Dahlonega   Consolidated Gold Mine—Mine tour

Dahlonega Gold Museum—Tells the story of the GA Gold Rush

Elberton   Elberton Granite Museum—Granite quarry and products

Helen   Gold Mine of Helen, GA—Mine tour

Macon   Museum of Arts and Science—Display of gems and minerals

Statesboro   Georgia Southern Museum—Collection of rocks and minerals from Georgia's highlands, Piedmont, and coastal regions

Tallapoosa   West Georgia Museum of Tallapoosa—Small collection of local minerals

Annual Events

Jasper   Pickens County Marble Festival—First weekend in October

HAWAII

Fee Dig Mines and Guide Services
>None

Museums and Mine Tours

Hawaii Nat'l Park   Thomas A. Jaggar Museum—Museum on vulcanology and seismology; tour of volcano

Hilo   Lyman House Memorial Museum—Rocks, minerals, gems

IDAHO

Fee Dig Mines and Guide Services

Moscow   3-D's Panhandle Gems and Garnet Queen Mine—Guide service, star garnet digging; trips including gold panning.

Spencer   Spencer Opal Mine—Pick through a stockpile for fire opal; pre-arranged digging at mine is a possibility

St. Maries   Emerald Creek Garnet Area—Dig for star garnets

Museums and Mine Tours

Caldwell   The Glen L. and Ruth M. Evans Gem and Mineral Collection—Agate, jasper, other gemstones, 2,000 cabochons

Orma J. Smith Museum of Natural History—Extensive collection of minerals

ILLINOIS

Fee Dig Mines and Guide Services
>None

Museums and Mine Tours

Chicago   The Field Museum—92-year-old gem exhibit

Elmhurst   Lizzadro Museum of Lapidary Art—1,300 pieces of cut and polished gems, fluorescent rocks, a birthstone display

Galena   Vinegar Hill Lead Mine and Museum—Mine tour and museum

Rock Island   Augustana Fryxell Geology Museum—Rock and mineral musuem

Rosiclare   The American Fluorite Museum—Story of Fluorospur Industry

Springfield   Illinois State Museum—Gems and minerals, Illinois specimens, birthstones, fluorescents, copper

West Frankfort   The National Coal Museum, Mine 25—Tour a shaft coal mine

INDIANA

Fee Dig Mines and Guide Services

Knightstown   Yogi Bear Jellystone Park Camping Resort—Midwestern gold prospecting

Museums and Mine Tours

Bedford   Land of Limestone Exhibition—History of Indiana Limestone industry

Fort Wayne   Indiana Purdue University at Fort Wayne—Hallway displays of minerals, meteorites, and rocks

Indianapolis   Indiana State Museum—Indiana and regional minerals

Richmond   Joseph Moore Museum of Natural History, Earlham College—Geology exhibit from local Ordovician limestone

IOWA

Fee Dig Mines and Guide Services

None

Museums and Mine Tours

Danville   Geode State Park—Display of geodes

Iowa City   University of Iowa—Displays on state geology

Sioux City   Sioux City Public Museum—Mineralogy exhibit

Waterloo   Grout Museum—Display of rocks and minerals

West Bend   Grotto of the Redemption—Grotto made of precious stones and gems

Winterset   Madison County Historical Society—Rock and mineral collection

KANSAS

Fee Dig Mines and Guide Services

None

Museums and Mine Tours

Ashland   Pioneer Krier Museum—Mineral exhibit

Greensburg   Pallasite Meteorite at the Big Well Museum—Meteorite strike site and 1,000-pound meteorite

McPherson   McPherson Museum—Meteorites

KENTUCKY

Fee Dig Mines and Guide Services
None

Museums and Mine Tours
Benham   Kentucky Coal Mine Museum—Displays on coal mining and formation of coal
Covington   Behringen-Crawford Museum—Display of gems and minerals
Lynch   Lynch Portal 31 Walking Tour—Walking tour of coal mining facilities
Marion   The Clement Mineral Museum—Display of gems and minerals

LOUISIANA

Fee Dig Mines and Guide Services
None

Museums and Mine Tours
New Orleans   Louisiana Nature Center—Small collection of gems and minerals
Shreveport   Louisiana State Exhibit Museum—Displays on mining and salt domes

MAINE

Fee Dig Mines and Guide Services
Albany   Bumpus Quarry—Collect garnet, albite, beryl, rose quartz, and black tourmaline
Bethel   Songo Pond Mine—Collect tourmaline and other ME gems and minerals
Poland   Poland Mining Camp—Collect tourmaline and other ME gems and minerals
West Paris Perham's of West Paris—Collect tourmaline and other ME gems and minerals

Museums and Mine Tours
Augusta   Maine State Museum—Gems and minerals of ME
West Paris Perham's of West Paris—ME gems and minerals; model of a feldspar quarry, model of a gem tourmaline pocket, fluorescents

Annual Events
Augusta   Maine Mineral Symposium—3rd weekend in May

MARYLAND

Fee Dig Mines and Guide Services
>None

Museums and Mine Tours
>None

MASSACHUSETTS

Fee Dig Mines and Guide Services
>None

Museums and Mine Tours

Amherst	Pratt Museum of Natural History—10,000 specimens; minerals from New England and around the world, meteorites
Cambridge	Harvard University Museum of Cultural and Natural History—Gems, minerals, ores, meteorites
Springfield	Springfield Science Museum—Minerals from around the world

MICHIGAN

Fee Dig Mines and Guide Services

Mohawk	Delaware Copper Mine—Search for souvenir copper

Museums and Mine Tours

Ann Arbor	Exhibit Museum of Natural History, University of Michigan—Exhibits of rocks and minerals
Bloomfield Hills	Cranbrook Institute of Science—5,000 minerals and crystals from around the world, including hiddenite, gold
Calumet	Mining Museum at Coppertown, U.S.A.—Exhibits on copper mining
Caspian	Iron County Museum and Park—Iron mining complex
Chelsea	Gerald E. Eddy Geology Center—MI rocks, minerals, crystals, and mining
Copper Harbor	Fort Wilkins State Park—History of copper mining in the area
Hancock	The Quincy Mining Company—Tour an underground copper mine
Houghton	The Seaman Mineral Museum—Crystal collection, minerals from the Lake Superior copper district
Iron Mountain	Iron Mountain Iron Mine—Iron mine tour
Lake Linden	Houghton County Historical Museum—Copper mining and refining equipment displays

Mohawk	Delaware Copper Mine—Mine tour
Mount Pleasant	Museum of Cultural and Natural History, Central Michigan University—MI rocks and minerals
Negaunee	Michigan Iron Industry Museum—Story of MI iron industry
Shelby	Shelby Man-Made Gemstones—Exhibits on producing artificial gems

MINNESOTA

Fee Dig Mines and Guide Services
None

Museums and Mine Tours
Calumet	Hill Annex Mine State Park—Tour an open pit iron mine
Chisholm	Ironworld Discovery Center—Iron industry taconite mining tours
	Minnesota Museum of Mining—Indoor and outdoor exhibits
	Taconite Mine Tours—Tour of an open-pit iron ore mine
Hibbing	Mahoning Hull-Rust Mine—Observe an open-pit iron mine
Pipestone	Pipestone National Monument—Tour a Native American pipestone quarry
Soudan	Soudan Underground Mine State Park—Tour an underground iron mine
Virginia	Mineview in the Sky—View an open-pit iron ore mine
	Iron Trails Conventions and Visitor's Bureau—Information on mine view sites

MISSISSIPPI

Fee Dig Mines and Guide Services
None

Museums and Mine Tours
Greenwood	Cottonlandia Museum—Rocks and minerals from around the world

MISSOURI

Fee Dig Mines and Guide Services
Alexandria	Sheffler Rock Shop—Dig geodes lined with crystals

Museums and Mine Tours

Golden   Golden Pioneer Museum—Large mineral exhibit

Joplin   Everett J. Richie Tri-State Mineral Museum—Story of area's lead and zinc mining

Kansas City   University of Missouri–Kansas City, Geosciences Museum—Local and regional specimens

Park Hills   Missouri Mines State Historic Site—1,100 minerals, ores, and rocks

Point Lookout Ralph Foster Museum, College of the Ozarks—Gemstone spheres and fluorescent minerals

Rolla   Mineral Museum, U. of Missouri, Rolla—3,500 minerals, ores, and rocks from 92 countries and 47 states

MONTANA

Fee Dig Mines and Guide Services

Alder   Red Rock Mine—Screen for garnets

Clinton   L◊E Guest Ranch Outfitters—Sapphire mining pack trips

Dillon   Crystal Park Recreational Mineral Collecting Area—Dig for quartz and amethyst crystal

Hamilton   Sapphire Studio—Sapphire mining "parties"

Helena   Spokane Bar Sapphire Mine and Gold Fever Rock Shop—Dig and screen for sapphires and other gems and minerals

Philipsburg   Gem Mountain—search for sapphires

                  Sapphire Gallery—Wash bags of gravel to look for sapphires

Museums and Mine Tours

Butte   Anselmo Mine Yard—Tour of mining facilities and history of area mining

                  The Berkeley Pit—Observation point for closed open-pit copper mine

                  Butte-Silver Bow Visitors and Transportation Center—Presents information on area geology and its mining, including local gold and silver mining

                  Mineral Museum, Montana College of Mineral Science and Technology—Gold, fluorescents, and minerals from Butte and MT

                  World Museum of Mining and 1899 Mining Camp—Tour of surface facilities of former silver and zinc mine

Ekalaka   Carter County Museum—Fluorescent mineral display

Lewistown   Central Montana Museum—Rocks, minerals, and yogo sapphires

NEBRASKA

Fee Dig Mines and Guide Services
>None

Museums and Mine Tours

Hastings Hastings Museum—Minerals, rocks, fluorescent minerals, and translucent slabs

Lincoln University of Nebraska State Museum—Displays of rocks, minerals and fluorescent rocks

NEVADA

Fee Dig Mines and Guide Services

Denio Rainbow Ridge Opal Mine—Tailings digging for wood opal
Royal Peacock Opal Mine, Inc.—Dig black and fire opal

Ely Garnet Fields Rockhound Area—Hunt for garnets

Gerlach Royal Rainbow Fire Opal Mine—Dig for fire opal

Museums and Mine Tours

Las Vegas Nevada State Museum and Historical Society—Natural history of Nevada

Virginia City Chollar Mine—Underground mine tour (gold and silver mine)

NEW HAMPSHIRE

Fee Dig Mines and Guide Services

Grafton Ruggles Mine—Collect up to 150 different minerals

Museums and Mine Tours

Dover The Woodman Institute—1,300 specimens, including local rocks

NEW JERSEY

Fee Dig Mines and Guide Services

Cape May Cape May Welcome Center—Hunt for Cape May "diamonds"

Franklin Franklin Mineral Museum and Buckwheat Dump—Tailings diggings for fluorescent minerals

Museums and Mine Tours

Franklin Franklin Mineral Museum—Minerals, rocks, local and worldwide fluorescents

Monroe Township	Displayworld's Stone Museum—Minerals, hands-on exhibits
Morristown	Morristown Museum—Specimens from five continents
New Brunswick	Rutgers Geology Museum—Specimens from the zinc deposit at Franklin and the zeolite deposits from Paterson, meteorites
Ogdensburg	Sterling Hill Mine and Museum—Tour old zinc mine
Paterson	The Paterson Museum—Specimens from local basalt flows and basalt flow in the Poona region of India, minerals from NJ and around the world
Rutherford	Meadowland Museum—Fluorescent minerals, quartz, minerals from NJ
Trenton	New Jersey State Museum—Minerals and rocks, including fluorescents and magnetite ore

Annual Events

Franklin	New Jersey Earth Science Association Gem and Mineral Show and Outdoor Swap & Sell—Late April

NEW MEXICO

Fee Dig Mines and Guide Services

Bingham	Blanchard Mines—Collect over 84 different kinds of minerals in a former lead mine
Deming	Rockhound State Park—collect a variety of semiprecious stones
Dixon	Harding Mine—Harding pegmatite has yielded over 50 minerals
Magdalena	Bill's Gems & Minerals—Collect copper and iron minerals at mine dumps

Museums and Mine Tours

Albuquerque	Geology Museum, University of New Mexico—Displays of NM minerals and geology
	Institute of Meteoritics, University of New Mexico—Meteorites
	New Mexico Museum of Natural History and Science—3,000 specimens with a focus on NM and the southwestern U.S.
	The Turquoise Museum—Turquoise museum
Socorro	New Mexico Bureau of Mines and Mineral Resources—10,000 specimens of minerals from NM, the U.S., and the world

Annual Events

Socorro	New Mexico Mineral Symposium

NEW YORK

Fee Dig Mines and Guide Services

Herkimer   Herkimer Diamond Mine and KOA Kampground—Dig for Herkimer "Diamonds"

Little Falls   Treasure Mountain Diamond Mine—Dig for Herkimer "Diamonds"

Middleville   Ace of Diamonds Mine and Campground—Prospect for Herkimer "Diamonds"

North River   Barton Mines—Hunt for garnets

St. Johnsville Crystal Grove Diamond Mine and Campground—Dig for Herkimer "Diamonds"

Museums and Mine Tours

Albany   New York State Museum—Minerals from New York

Hicksville   The Hicksville Gregory Museum—9,000 specimens form the major minerals groups; also NJ zeolites, Herkimer "diamonds," fluorescents

New York   American Museum of Natural History—Gems, meteorites; emphasis on exceptional specimens from the U.S.

Pawling   The Gunnison Natural History Museum—Minerals

NORTH CAROLINA

Fee Dig Mines and Guide Services

Almond   Nantahala Gorge Ruby Mine—Sluice for rubies, sapphires, amethyst, topaz, garnet, citrine, smoky quartz

Canton   Old Pressley Sapphire Mine—Sluice for sapphires

Cherokee   Smoky Mountain Gold & Ruby Mine—Sluice for gold and gems

Franklin   Cherokee Ruby and Sapphire Mine—Sluice for rubies, sapphires, garnets, moonstones, rutile, sillimanite

Cowee Mountain Ruby Mine—Sluice for rubies, sapphires, garnets, tourmaline, smoky quartz, amethyst, citrine, moonstone, topaz

Gold City Gem Mine—Sluice for rubies, sapphires, garnets, emeralds, tourmaline, smoky quartz, amethyst, citrine, moonstone, topaz

Jackson Hole—Sluice for rubies, sapphire, garnets, tourmaline, smoky quartz, amethyst, citrine, moonstone, topaz

Mason Mountain Rhodolite and Ruby Mine and Cowee Gift Shop—Sluice for rhodolite, rubies, sapphires, garnets, kyanite, crystal quartz, smoky quartz, moonstones

Masons Ruby and Sapphire Mine—Dig and sluice for sapphires (all colors), pink and red rubies

	Moonstone Gem Mine—Sluice for rhodolite, rubies, sapphires, garnets, other precious stones
	The Old Cardinal Gem Mine—Sluice for rare native rhodolite, rubies, sapphires, garnets, moonstones, topaz, other precious stones
	Rocky Face Gem Mine—Sluice for rubies, rhodolite garnets
	Rose Creek Mine, Campground, Trout Pond, and Rock Shop—Sluice for rubies, sapphires, garnets, moonstones, amethysts, smoky quartz, citrine, rose quartz, topaz
	Sheffield Mine—Sluice for rubies, sapphires, enriched material from around the world
Hiddenite	Emerald Hollow Mine, Hiddenite Gems, Inc.—Rutile, sapphires, garnets, monazite, hiddenite, smoky quartz, tourmaline, clear quartz, aquamarine, sillimanite
Little Switzerland	Blue Ridge Gemstone Mine & Campground—Sapphire, emeralds, rubies, aquamarine, tourmaline, topaz, garnets, amethysts, lepidolite, citrine, moonstone, kyanite, and rose, clear, rutilated, and smoky quartz
	Emerald Village—Sapphire, emeralds, rubies, aquamarine, tourmaline, topaz, garnets, amethysts, lepidolite, citrine, beryl, moonstone, kyanite, and rose, clear, rutilated, and smoky quartz
Marion	The Lucky Strike—Gems and gold panning
	Carolina Emerald Mine and Vein Mountain Gold Camp—Mine for gold, emerald, aquamarine, moonstone, feldspar crystals, garnets, smoky, rose, blue and clear quartz, and tourmaline
New London	Cotton Patch Gold Mine—Gold panning
Spruce Pine	Gem Mountain Gemstone Mine—Sapphires, crabtree emeralds, rubies, Wiseman aquamarine
	Rio Doce Gem Mine—Sapphires, emeralds, rubies, aquamarine, tourmaline, topaz, garnets, amethysts, lepidolite, citrine, beryl, moonstone, kyanite, and rose, clear, rutilated, and smoky quartz
	Rock Mine Tours and Gift Shop—Dig for emeralds, aquamarine, golden beryl, feldspar, pink feldspar, star garnets, biotite, olivine, moonstone, thulite, and black tourmaline
	Spruce Pine Gem and Gold Mine—Sapphires, emeralds, rubies, aquamarine, tourmaline, topaz, garnets, amethysts, lepidolite, citrine, beryl, moonstone, kyanite, and rose, clear, rutilated, and smoky quartz
Stanfield	Reed Gold Mine Historic Site—Gold panning
Union Mills	Thermal City Gold Mining Company—Gold panning

Museums and Mine Tours

Asheville	Colburn Gem & Mineral Museum—Collection of mineral specimens from NC and the world

Franklin	Franklin Gem and Mineral Museum—Specimens from NC and around the world
	Ruby City Gems—Specimens from NC and around the world
Gastonia	Schiele Museum—North Carolina gems and minerals
Greensboro	Natural Science Center of Greensboro—Specimens from NC and around the world
Hendersonville	Mineral and Lapidary Museum of Hendersonville, Inc.—Minerals and lapidary arts
Linville	Grandfather Mountain Nature Museum—Specimens from NC
Little Switzerland	North Carolina Mining Museum and Mine Tour—tour a closed feldspar mine
Spruce Pine	Museum of North Carolina Minerals—Specimens primarily from local mines
Stanfield	Reed Gold Mine Historic Site—Gold mine tour

Annual Events

Franklin	Macon County Gemboree—3rd weekend in July
	"Leaf Looker" Gemboree—2nd weekend in October
Spruce Pine	Original NC Mineral and Gem Festival—4 days at the beginning of August

NORTH DAKOTA

Fee Dig Mines and Guide Services
        None

Museums and Mine Tours

Dickinson	Dakota Dinosaur Museum—Rocks and minerals, including borax from CA, turquoise from AZ, fluorescents, aurora crystals from AR

OHIO

Fee Dig Mines and Guide Services

Hopewell	Hidden Springs Ranch—Dig for flint (groups only)
	Nethers Flint—Dig for flint

Museums and Mine Tours

Cleveland	The Cleveland Museum of Natural History—The Wade Gallery of Gems and Minerals has over 1,500 gems and minerals

Columbus	Orton Geological Museum—Rocks and minerals from OH and the world
Dayton	Boonshoft Museum of Discovery—Minerals and crystals
Glenford	Flint Ridge State Memorial—Ancient flint quarrying
Lima	Allen County Museum—Rock and mineral exhibit

OKLAHOMA

Fee Dig Mines and Guide Services
Jet	Salt Plains National Wildlife Refuge—Digging for selenite crystals
Kenton	Black Mesa Bed & Breakfast—Rockhounding on a working cattle ranch
	Howard Layton Ranch—Rockhounding on a working cattle ranch

Museums and Mine Tours
Coalgate	Coal Country Mining and Historical Museum—Mining museum
Enid	The Mr. and Mrs. Dan Midgley Museum—Rock and mineral collection predominantly from OK and the TX shoreline
Noble	Timberlake Rose Rock Museum—Displays of barite roses
Picher	Picher Mining Museum—Lead and zinc mining
Tulsa	Elsing Museum—Gems and minerals

Annual Events
| Cherokee | The Crystal Festival and Selenite Crystal Dig—First Saturday in May |
| Noble | Annual Rose Rock Festival—First Saturday in May |

OREGON

Fee Dig Mines and Guide Services
Madras	Richards Recreational Ranch—Dig for thundereggs, agate
Mitchell	Lucky Strike Geodes—Dig for thundereggs (picture jasper)
Yachats	Beachcombing—Collect agates and jaspers

Museums and Mine Tours
Central Point	Crater Rock Museum—Minerals, thundereggs, fossils, geodes, cut and polished gemstones
Redmond	Peterson's Rock Garden—Unusual rock specimens, fluorescent display
Sumpter	Sumpter Valley Dredge State Historical Heritage Area—View a gold dredge, tour historic gold mine towns

Annual Events
Cottage Grove Bohemia Mining Days—Four days in July, gold panning and exposition
Prineville Rockhounds Pow-Wow—mid-June

PENNSYLVANIA

Fee Dig Mines and Guide Services
    None

Museums and Mine Tours
Ashland Museum of Anthracite Mining—Story of anthracite coal
    Pioneer Tunnel Coal Mine—Tour an anthracite coal mine
Bryn Mawr Museum, Department of Geology, Bryn Mawr College—Rotating display of 1,500 minerals from collection of 23,500 specimens
Carlisle Rennie Geology Museum, Dickinson College—Gem and mineral display
Harrisburg State Museum of Pennsylvania—Geology of everyday products
Lancaster North Museum of Natural History and Science—Worldwide specimens with a focus on Lancaster County
Media Delaware County Institute of Science—Minerals from around the world
Patton Seldom Seen Mine—Tour a bituminous coal mine
Philadelphia Wagner Free Institute of Science—Rocks and minerals
Pittsburgh Carnegie Museum of Natural History—Gems and minerals
Scranton Anthracite Museum Complex—Several anthracite coal–related attractions, including mine tours and museums
Tarentum Tour-Ed Mine—Bituminous coal mine tour
University Park College of Earth and Mineral Sciences, Penn State University—Minerals
Waynesburg Paul R. Stewart Museum, Waynesburg College—Outstanding mineral collection
West Chester Geology Museum, West Chester University—Specimens from Chester County, fluorescent specimens
Wilkes-Barre Wyoming Historical & Geological Society Museum—Displays on anthracite coal mining
Windber Windber Coal Heritage Center—Exhibits present the heritage of coal mining

Annual Events

Pittsburgh　　The Carnegie Museum of Natural History Gem & Mineral Show—last weekend in August

University Park　Mineral Symposium—Three days in May

RHODE ISLAND

Fee Dig Mines and Guide Services
　　　　None

Museums and Mine Tours

Providence　　Museum of Natural History and Planetarium—Rocks and minerals

SOUTH CAROLINA

Fee Dig Mines and Guide Services
　　　　None

Museums and Mine Tours

Charleston　　Charleston Museum—Small display of gems and minerals

Clemson　　　Bob Campbell Geology Museum—Minerals, meteorites, faceted stones

Columbia　　McKissick Museum, University of South Carolina Campus—Exhibits on geology and gemstones

　　　　　　South Carolina State Museum—Small display of rocks and minerals

SOUTH DAKOTA

Fee Dig Mines and Guide Services

Deadwood　　Broken Boot Gold Mine—Pan for gold

Keystone　　Big Thunder Gold Mine—Pan for gold

Lead　　　　Black Hills Mining Museum—Pan for gold

Wall　　　　Buffalo Gap National Grasslands—Hunt for agates

Museums and Mine Tours

Deadwood　　Broken Boot Gold Mine—Gold mine tour

Keystone　　Big Thunder Gold Mine—Underground mine tour

Lead　　　　Black Hills Mining Museum—Simulated underground mine tour

　　　　　　Homestead Visitors Center—Gold mining displays

Murdo　　　National Rockhound and Lapidary Hall of Fame—Gems and minerals

Rapid City　South Dakota School of Mines and Technology—Local minerals

TENNESSEE

Fee Dig Mines and Guide Services
Ducktown   Burra Burra Mine—Dig for garnets, pyrite, chalcopyrite, pyrrhotite, actinolite

Museums and Mine Tours
Johnson City   Hands On! Regional Museum—Simulated coal mine
Knoxville   McClung Museum—Geology of Tennessee
Memphis   Memphis Pink Palace Museum—Geology and minerals from famous mid-South localities

TEXAS

Fee Dig Mines and Guide Services
Alpine   Stillwell Ranch—Hunt for agate and jasper
Woodward Ranch—Hunt for agate, precious opal, and others
Mason   Hoffman Ranch—Hunt for topaz
Seaquist Ranch—Hunt for topaz
Three Rivers   House Ranch—Hunt for agate

Museums and Mine Tours
Austin   Texas Memorial Museum—Gems and minerals
Canyon   Panhandle Plains Historical Museum—Gems and minerals from the TX panhandle; meteorites
Fort Stockton   Annie Riggs Memorial Museum—Rocks and minerals of Pecos County and the Big Bend area
Fritch   Alibates Flint Quarries—View ancient flint quarries
Marble Falls   Granite Mountain—View marble mining operations
McKinney   The Heard Natural Science Museum and Wildlife Sanctuary—Rocks and minerals
Odessa   Odessa Meteor Crater—Meteorite crater

Annual Events
Alpine   Alpine Gem Show—mid-April

UTAH

Fee Dig Mines and Guide Services
None

Museums and Mine Tours

Bingham Canyon Bingham Canyon Mine Visitors Center—Overlook for open-pit-copper mine

Eureka Tintec Mining Museum—Mineral display and mining artifacts

Helper Western Mining and Railroad Museum—Mining exhibits, simulated 1900 coal mine

Hyrum Hyrum City Museum—Display of fluorescent minerals

Lehi John Hutchings Museum of Natural History—Minerals linked to mining districts, display of uncut gems

Salt Lake City Utah Museum of Natural History—Mineral classification; UT ores and minerals, fluorescent minerals

VERMONT

Fee Dig Mines and Guide Services

None

Museums and Mine Tours

Barre Rock of Ages Corporation—Watch granite being quarried

Norwich Montshire Museum of Science—Fluorescent minerals

Proctor Vermont Marble Exhibit—Story of marble

VIRGINIA

Fee Dig Mines and Guide Services

Amelia Dick R. Boyles—Dig for beryl

Morefield Gem Mine—Dig and sluice for garnet, quartz, topaz, and many others

Stuart Fairy Stone State Park—Hunt for staurolite crystals (fairy stones)

Museums and Mine Tours

Blocksburg Virginia Tech Museum of Geological Sciences—Large display of Virginia minerals

Martinsville Virginia Museum of Natural History—Minerals and mining exhibits

WASHINGTON

Fee Dig Mines and Guide Services

Ravensdale Bob Jackson's Geology Adventures—Field trips: collect quartz, garnets, topaz, and others

Museums and Mine Tours

Castle Rock   Mount St. Helens National Volcanic Monument—Focus on geology

Ellensburg   Kittitas County Historical Museum and Society—Polished rocks

Pullman   Washington State University—Silicified wood, minerals

Seattle   Burke Museum of Natural History and Culture—Rocks, minerals, the geology of Washington, and a walk-through volcano

WEST VIRGINIA

Fee Dig Mines and Guide Services
None

Museums and Mine Tours
Beckley   The Beckley Exhibition Coal Mine—Tour a bituminous coal mine

WISCONSIN

Fee Dig Mines and Guide Services
None

Museums and Mine Tours

Dodgeville   The Museum of Minerals and Crystals—Local mineral specimens, specimens from around the world

Hurley   Iron County Historical Museum—History of area mining, also, last remaining mine head frame in Wisconsin

Madison   Geology Museum, University of Wisconsin at Madison—Minerals, fluorescent minerals, model of Wisconsin cave

Milwaukee   Milwaukee Public Museum—Displays of geological specimens
University of Wisconsin at Milwaukee—Minerals

Platteville   The Mining Museum—Lead and zinc mining in the upper Mississippi Valley

Stevens Point   Museum of Natural History—University of Wisconsin—Stevens Point rock and mineral display

WYOMING

Fee Dig Mines and Guide Services
Shell   Trapper Galloway Ranch—Dig for moss agate

Museums and Mine Tours
Casper   Tate Geological Museum—Rocks and minerals, including WY jade, and fluorescent minerals

Cheyenne	Wyoming State Museum—Minerals of Wyoming, coal "Swamp"
Laramie	Geological Museum, University of Wyoming—Rocks and minerals, fluorescent minerals from WY
Rock River	Rock River Museum—Fluorescent mineral display
Saritoga	Saritoga Museum—Minerals from around the world, local geology
Worland	Washaki Museum—Agates, crystals

Annual Events

Casper	Tate Geological Museum Symposium on Wyoming Geology—June

Index by Gems and Minerals

This index lists all the gems and minerals that can be found at fee dig mines in the U.S., and shows the city and state where the mine is located. To use the index, look up the gem or mineral you are interested in, and note the states and cities where they are located. Then go to the state and city to find the name of the mine, and information about the mine.

The following notes provide additional information:

(#)   A number in parentheses is the number of mines in that town that have that gem or mineral.

(*)   Gem or mineral is found in the state, but the mine may also add material to the ore. Check with the individual mine for confirmation.

(FT) Field trip.

(GS) Guide service (location listed is the location of the guide service, not necessarily the location of the gems or minerals being collected).

(I)   Mineral has been identified at the mine site but may be difficult to find.

(M)   Museum that allows collection of one specimen as a souvenir.

(MM) Micromount (a very small crystal which, when viewed under a microscope or magnifying glass, is found to be a high-quality crystal).

(O)   Available at mine but comes from other mines.

(R)   Can be found, but is rare.

(S)   Not the main gem or mineral for which the site is known.

(SA) "Salted" or enriched gem or mineral.

(U)   Unique to the site.

(Y)   Yearly collecting event.

Actinolite Tennessee: Ducktown

Agate Arkansas: Murfreesboro (S); Iowa: Bonaporte; Montana: Helena (S); Nevada: Gerlach; New Mexico: Deming (GS); Oklahoma: Kenton (2); Oregon: Yachats; South Dakota: Wall; Texas: Three Rivers; Virginia: Amelia
  Banded agate Texas: Alpine
  Fire agate California: Palo Verde
  Iris agate Texas: Alpine

Ledge agate Oregon: Madras
Moss agate Oregon: Madras, Mitchell; Texas: Alpine (2); Wyoming: Shell
Polka-dot jasp-agate Oregon: Madras
Plume agate Oregon: Madras
Pompom agate Texas: Alpine
Rainbow agate Oregon: Madras
Red plume agate Texas: Alpine

Albite Maine: Albany, Poland (GS), West Paris; New Hampshire: Grafton (I); New Mexico: Dixon

Albite (Cleavelandite Var.) Maine: Poland (GS)

Amazonite Virginia: Amelia

Amber Texas: Mason (R); Washington: Ravensdale (GS)

Amethyst Arkansas: Murfreesboro (S); Georgia: Cleveland, Helen (SA); Maine: Bethel (R), West Paris; Montana: Dillon; New Hampshire: Grafton (I); New Mexico: Bingham; North Carolina (*): Almond, Cherokee, Franklin (5), Little Switzerland, Spruce Pine (3)
Crystal scepters Nevada: Sun Valley (GS)

Amblygonite Maine: West Paris

Amphibolite New Hampshire: Grafton (I)

Apatite California: Palo Verde (MM); Maine: Bethel, Poland (GS), West Paris; New Hampshire: Grafton; New Mexico, Dixon
Fluorapatite Maine: Poland (GS)
Green apatite Maine: West Paris
Hydroxylapatite Maine: Poland (GS)
Purple apatite Maine: West Paris

Aplite New Hampshire: Grafton (I)

Aquamarine Maine: Bethel, Poland (GS); New Hampshire: Grafton (I); North Carolina (*): Hiddenite, Little Switzerland (2), Marion, Spruce Pine (2) (FT)
Brushy Creek aquamarine North Carolina: Spruce Pine (1) (FT)
Weisman aquamarine North Carolina: Spruce Pine (1) (FT)

Arsenopyrite Maine: Poland (GS)

Augelite Maine: Poland (GS)

Aurichalcite New Mexico: Bingham, Magdalena

Autenite Maine: Poland (GS); New Hampshire: Grafton (I)

Azurite New Mexico: Magdalena; Utah: Moab (GS)

Barite Arkansas: Murfreesboro (S); California: Palo Verde (MM); Georgia: Lincolnton; New Mexico: Bingham; Washington: Ravensdale (GS)

Beraumite Maine: Poland (GS)

Bermanite Maine: Poland (GS)

Bertrandite Maine: Poland (GS), West Paris

Bertranite New Hampshire: Grafton (I)

Beryl Maine: Albany, Poland (GS), West Paris; New Mexico, Dixon; North Carolina (*): Little Switzerland (2), Spruce Pine (2); South Dakota: Custer (GS); Virginia: Amelia (2)
  Aqua beryl New Hampshire: Grafton (I)
  Blue beryl (see also aquamarine) New Hampshire: Grafton (I)
  Golden beryl North Carolina: Spruce Pine (FT); New Hampshire: Grafton (I)

Beryllonite Maine: Poland (GS), West Paris

Biotite New Hampshire: Grafton (I); North Carolina: Spruce Pine

Borate California: Boron (Y)

Bornite New Hampshire: Grafton (I)

Brazilianite Maine: Poland (GS)

Brochantite New Mexico: Bingham

Calcite Arkansas: Murfreesboro (S); California: Palo Verde (MM); New Hampshire: Grafton; New Mexico: Bingham; Virginia: Amelia

Cape May "diamonds" See Quartz

Casserite Maine: Poland (GS)

Cassiterite Maine: West Paris

Cerussite New Mexico: Bingham

Chalcedony New Mexico: Deming

Chalcopyrite Tennessee: Ducktown

Childrenite Maine: Poland (GS)

Chrysoberyl Maine: West Paris; New Hampshire: Grafton (I)

Chrysocolla New Mexico: Bingham

Citrine Georgia: Helen (SA); North Carolina (SA): Almond, Cherokee, Franklin (6), Little Switzerland, Spruce Pine (3)

Clarkite New Hampshire: Grafton (I)

Clevelandite Maine: West Paris; New Hampshire: Grafton (I); New Mexico: Dixon

Clinoptilolite California: Palo Verde (MM)

Columbite New Hampshire: Grafton (I); Maine: Bethel, Poland (GS), West Paris

Compotite New Hampshire: Grafton (I)

Cookeite Maine: West Paris

Copper minerals Michigan: Mohawk (M); New Mexico: Magdalena

Covellite New Mexico: Bingham

Crandalite Georgia: Lincolnton

Cryolite New Hampshire: Grafton (I)

Cuprite New Mexico: Bingham

Cymatolite New Hampshire: Grafton (I)

Dendrites Nevada: Gerlach; New Hampshire: Grafton (I)

Diadochite Maine: Poland (GS)

Diamond Arkansas: Murfreesboro

Dickinsonite Maine: Poland (GS)

Earlshannonite Maine: Poland (GS)

Elbaite See listing under Tourmaline

Emerald Georgia: Cleveland, Dahlonega (SA); North Carolina (*): Cherokee, Franklin, Hiddenite, Little Switzerland (2), Marion, Spruce Pine (2)
   Crabtree Emerald North Carolina: Spruce Pine

Eosphorite Maine: Poland (GS)

Fairfieldite Maine: Poland (GS)

Fairy stones (See Staurolite crystals)

Feldspar Colorado: Lake George; New Hampshire: Grafton (I); North Carolina: Marion, Spruce Pine; Virginia: Amelia
   Albite feldspar Maine: Bethel

Flint Ohio: Hopewell (2)

Fluoroapatite New Hampshire: Grafton (I)

Fluorescent minerals New Jersey: Franklin; North Carolina: Little Switzerland; Washington: Ravensdale (GS)

Fluorite California: Palo Verde (MM); New Mexico: Bingham, Socorro (Y); South Dakota: Custer (GS); Virginia: Amelia; Washington: Ravensdale (GS)

Gahnite (spinel) Maine: Poland (GS), West Paris

Gainsite Maine: Poland (GS)

Galena New Mexico: Bingham

Garnets Georgia: Dahlonega (SA), Helen (SA); Idaho: St. Maries; Maine: Albany, Bethel, Poland (GS), West Paris (3); Montana: Alder, Helena (S); New Hampshire: Grafton (I); New Mexico: Dixon; New York: North River; North Carolina (*): Almond, Cherokee, Franklin (7), Hiddenite, Little Switzerland (2), Marion, Spruce Pine (3) (FT); Nevada: Ely; Tennessee: Ducktown; Washington: Ravensdale (GS)
   Almandine garnets Maine: Poland (GS); Nevada: Ely
   Pyrope garnets North Carolina: Franklin
   Rhodolite garnets North Carolina: Franklin (5)

Garnets, Star Idaho: Moscow (GS), St. Maries

Geodes Missouri: Alexandria; New Mexico: Deming
Lined with:
Agate, blue New Mexico: Deming
Aragonite Missouri: Alexandria
Barites Missouri: Alexandria
Chalcedony New Mexico: Deming
Dolomite Missouri: Alexandria
Goethite Missouri: Alexandria
Hematite Missouri: Alexandria
Kaoline Missouri: Alexandria
Opal, common New Mexico: Deming
Quartz New Mexico: Deming
Selenite needles Missouri: Alexandria
Sphalerite Missouri: Alexandria

Gold (*) Alaska: Fairbanks (3); Arizona: Apache Junction, Goldfield; California: Angels Camp (GS), Coloma, Columbia, Jackson, Mariposa, Nevada City, Pine Grove, Placerville; Colorado: Idaho Springs (2); Georgia: Cleveland, Dahlonega (2), Helen; Idaho: Moscow (GS); Indiana: Knightstown; Montana: Alder (O), Helena; North Carolina: Cherokee, Marion, New London, Stanfield, Union Mills; South Dakota: Deadwood, Keystone, Lead

Goshenite Colorado: Lake George

Goyazite Maine: Poland (GS)

Graftonite Maine: Poland (GS); New Hampshire: Grafton (I)

Gummite New Hampshire: Grafton (I)

Gypsum, curved California: Palo Verde (MM)

Hedenburgite New Mexico: Magdalena

Hematite Georgia: Lincolnton; Montana: Helena; New Mexico: Magdalena

Hemimorphite New Mexico: Bingham

Herderite, hydroxyl Maine: Bethel, Poland (GS), West Paris

Herkimer "diamonds" See Quartz

Heterosite Maine: Poland (GS)

Hiddenite (spodumene) North Carolina: Hiddenite

Hureaylite Maine: Poland (GS)

Iron minerals New Mexico: Magdalena

Iron ore Michigan: Iron Mountain (M)

Jade California: Pine Grove

Jadite Montana: Helena (S)

Jahnsite Maine: Poland (GS)

Jasper Arkansas: Murfreesboro (S); California: Pine Grove; Montana: Helena (S); Oklahoma: Kenton; Oregon: Madras, Yachats; Texas: Alpine
   Brown jasper New Mexico: Deming
   Chocolate jasper New Mexico: Deming
   Orange jasper New Mexico: Deming
   Picture jasper Oregon: Mitchell
   Pink jasper New Mexico: Deming
   Variegated jasper New Mexico: Deming
   Yellow jasper New Mexico: Deming

Jarosite Georgia: Lincolnton; New Mexico: Bingham

Kaolinite Maine: Poland (GS)

Kasolite New Hampshire: Grafton (I)

Kosnarite Maine: Poland (GS)

Kyanite Georgia: Lincolnton; North Carolina (*): Franklin, Little Switzerland

Labradorite Texas: Alpine

Lake County "diamonds" See Quartz

Landsite Maine: Poland (GS)

Laueite Maine: Poland (GS)

Lazulite Georgia: Lincolnton

Lepidolite Maine: Poland (GS), West Paris; New Mexico: Dixon; North Carolina (*): Little Switzerland
   Lemon Yellow Lepidolite New Hampshire: Grafton (I)

Lepidomelane New Hampshire: Grafton (I)

Linarite New Mexico: Bingham

Lithiophyllite Maine: Poland (GS); New Hampshire: Grafton (I)

Lollingite Maine: Poland (GS)

Ludlamite Maine: Poland (GS)

Magnesium oxide See Psilomellane

Magnesium oxide minerals New Mexico: Deming

Malachite New Mexico: Magdalena; Utah: Moab (GS)

Manganapatite New Hampshire: Grafton (I)

Manganese minerals New Mexico: Deming

Manganese oxide minerals New Mexico: Deming

Marcasite New Hampshire: Grafton (I)

McCrillisite Maine: Poland (GS)

Mica Maine: Poland (GS), West Paris; New Hampshire: Grafton (I); South Dakota: Custer (GS); Virginia: Amelia

Microcline Maine: Poland (GS)

Microlite New Mexico: Dixon

Mitridatite Maine: Poland (GS)

Molybdenite New Hampshire: Grafton

Montebrasite Maine: Poland (GS)

Montmorillonite Maine: Poland (GS), West Paris; New Hampshire: Grafton (I)

Monzaite Maine: Poland (GS)

Moonstone North Carolina (*): Franklin (7), Little Switzerland, Marion, Spruce Pine

Moraesite Maine: Poland (GS)

Murdochite New Mexico: Bingham

Muscovite Georgia: Lincolnton; New Hampshire: Grafton (I); New Mexico: Dixon

Olivine North Carolina: Spruce Pine

Opal
    Black opal Nevada: Orovado
    Common opal New Mexico: Deming
    Fire opal Nevada: Gerlach, Orovado
    Hyalite opal Maine: Bethel
    Precious opal Idaho: Spencer; Texas: Alpine
    Wood opal Nevada: Denio

Orthoclase Maine: Poland (GS)

Perhamite Maine: Poland (GS)

Parsonite New Hampshire: Grafton (I)

Perlite (black to gray) New Mexico: Deming

Peridot Arkansas: Murfreesboro (S); North Carolina (*): Franklin

Petalite Maine: Poland (GS), West Paris

Phenakite Virginia: Amelia

Phosphosiderite Georgia: Lincolnton; Maine: Poland (GS)

Phosphouranylite Maine: Poland (GS)

Phosphyanylite New Hampshire: Grafton (I)

Pitch Stone with seams of red & brown New Mexico: Deming

Plattnerite New Mexico: Bingham

Pollucite Maine: Poland (GS), West Paris

Psilomelane New Hampshire: Grafton (I)

Purpurite Maine: Poland (GS); New Hampshire: Grafton (I)

Pyrite Georgia: Lincolnton; Maine: Bethel, Poland (GS); New Hampshire: Grafton (I); New Mexico: Magdalena; Tennessee: Ducktown; Virginia: Amelia; Washington: Ravensdale (GS)

Pyrophyllite Georgia: Lincolnton

Pyrrhotite New Hampshire: Grafton (I); Tennessee: Ducktown

Quartz Arkansas: Hot Springs, Jessieville, Mt. Ida (7) (Y), Murfreesboro (S), Paron; California: Pine Grove; Colorado: Lake George; Georgia: Lincolnton; Maine: Poland (GS); Montana: Dillon, Helena (S); New Hampshire: Grafton; New Mexico: Bingham, Deming, Dixon, Socorro (Y); Texas: Alpine; Virginia: Amelia; Washington: Ravensdale (GS)

> **Blue** Georgia: Lincolnton; North Carolina: Marion
> **Clear** North Carolina (*): Franklin, Hiddenite, Little Switzerland, Marion, Spruce Pine
> **Milky** Maine: Bethel
> **Orange** Maine: West Paris
> **Parallel growth** Maine: West Paris
> **Pseudocubic crystals** Maine: West Paris
> **Rose** Georgia: Helen (SA); Maine: Albany, West Paris; New Hampshire: Grafton (I); North Carolina (*): Franklin, Little Switzerland, Marion
> **Rose (gem quality)** Maine: West Paris
> **Rutilated** North Carolina (*): Little Switzerland, Spruce Pine
> **Smoky** Georgia: Helen (SA); Maine: Bethel, West Paris; New Hampshire: Grafton (I); North Carolina (*): Almond, Cherokee, Franklin (6), Hiddenite, Little Switzerland (2), Marion, Spruce Pine (2)
> **Smoky (gem quality)** Maine: West Paris

Quartz "diamonds"
> **Lake Co. "diamonds" (moon tears)** California: Lake County
> **Cape May "diamonds"** New Jersey: Cape May
> **Herkimer "diamonds"** New York: Herkimer, Little Falls, Middleville, St. Johnsville

Reddingite Maine: Poland (GS); New Hampshire: Grafton (I)

Rhodochrosite Maine: Poland (GS)

Rhodolite (garnet) North Carolina: Franklin (2)

Rochbridgeite Maine: Poland (GS)

Rose rocks See Barite Rose

Rubies California: Pine Grove; Georgia: Cleveland, Dahlonega (SA); Montana: Helena (R); North Carolina (*): Almond, Cherokee, Franklin (13), Little Switzerland (2), Spruce Pine (3)

Rutile Georgia: Lincolnton; Maine: Bethel, Poland (GS); North Carolina: Franklin (2), Hiddenite; Virginia: Amelia

Safflorite New Hampshire: Grafton (I)

Sapphires Georgia: Cleveland, Dahlonega (SA); Montana: Alder (O), Clinton (GS), Gem Mountain, Hamilton, Helena (2), Philipsburg; North Carolina (*): Almond, Canton, Cherokee, Franklin (13), Hiddenite, Little Switzerland (2), Spruce Pine

Scheelite Maine: West Paris

Selenite crystals New Mexico: Bingham; Oklahoma: Jet (Y)

Serpentine Montana: Helena (S)

Siderite Maine: Bethel

Silica minerals New Mexico: Deming

Sillimanite New Hampshire: Grafton (I); North Carolina (*): Franklin (2), Hiddenite

Smithsonite New Mexico: Bingham, Magdalena, Socorro (Y)

Spangolite New Mexico: Bingham

Spessartine New Mexico: Dixon

Spodumene Maine: Poland (GS), West Paris; New Mexico: Dixon
    Altered Spodumene Maine: West Paris
    Hiddenite North Carolina: Hiddenite

Staurolite New Hampshire: Grafton (I); Virginia: Stuart

Stewartite Maine: Poland (GS)

Strengite Georgia: Lincolnton

Strunzite Maine: Poland (GS)

Sulfur Georgia: Lincolnton

Switzerite Maine: Poland (GS)

Tantalite-Columbite New Mexico: Dixon; Virginia: Amelia

Thulite North Carolina: Spruce Pine

Thundereggs New Mexico: Deming; Oregon: Madras, Mitchell

Tobernite New Hampshire: Grafton (I)

Topaz Georgia: Cleveland, Helen (SA); Maine: Poland (GS); Montana: Helena (R); New Hampshire: Grafton (I); North Carolina (SA): Cherokee, Franklin (6), Little Switzerland (3), Spruce Pine (3); Texas: Mason (2); Virginia: Amelia
    Blue topaz Colorado: Lake George
    Blue/sherry bicolor Colorado: Lake George
    Phenakite crystals in topaz Colorado: Lake George (U)
    Pink topaz Washington: Ravensdale (GS)
    Sherry topaz Colorado: Lake George

Torberite Maine: Poland (GS)

Tourmaline Maine: Poland (GS), West Paris; North Carolina (*): Franklin (7), Hid-denite, Little Switzerland (3), Spruce Pine (3) (FT); Virginia: Amelia
  Black tourmaline Maine: Albany, Bethel, Poland (GS), West Paris; New Hamp-shire: Grafton (I)
  Gem tourmaline Maine: West Paris
  Green tourmaline Maine: West Paris

Triphyllite Maine: Poland (GS), West Paris; New Hampshire: Grafton (I)

Triplite Maine: Poland (GS)

Uralolite Maine: Poland (GS)

Uranite Maine: Poland (GS); New Hampshire: Grafton (I) (Species with gummite—world-famous)

Uranium minerals New Hampshire: Grafton (I)

Uranophane New Hampshire: Grafton (I)

Vandendriesscheite New Hampshire: Grafton (I)

Variscite Georgia: Lincolnton

Vesuvianite Maine: Poland (GS),West Paris (2)

Vivianite New Hampshire: Grafton (I)

Voelerkenite New Hampshire: Grafton (I)

Wardilite Maine: Poland (GS)

Whitlockite Maine: Poland (GS)

Whitmoreite Maine: Poland (GS)

Wodginite Maine: Poland (GS)

Wulfenite New Mexico: Bingham

Zircon Maine: Bethel, Poland (GS), West Paris; New Hampshire: Grafton (I)

Annual Events

JANUARY

Quartzite, AZ, Gem and Mineral Shows—Mid-January–mid-February

FEBRUARY

Tucson, AZ, Gem and Mineral Show—First two weeks in February

MARCH

Scottsdale, AZ, Minerals of Arizona Symposium—1 day in March each year, sponsored by the Arizona Mineral & Mining Museum Foundation and the Arizona Department of Mines & Mineral Resources

Boron, CA, Rock Bonanza—Weekend before Easter

APRIL

Alpine, TX, Alpine Gem Show—Mid-April

MAY

Cherokee, OK, The Crystal Festival and Selenite Crystal Dig—First Saturday in May

Noble, OK, Rose Rock Festival—First Saturday in May

Augusta, ME, Maine Mineral Symposium—Third weekend in May

University Park, PA, Mineral Symposium c/o Penn State Mineral Museum—3 days in May

JUNE

Prineville, OR, Rockhounds Pow-Wow—Mid-June

Casper, WY, Tate Geological Museum Symposium on Wyoming Geology

JULY

Franklin, NC, Macon County Gemboree—Third weekend in July

Cottage Grove, OR, Bohemia Mining Days—Four days in July

AUGUST

Spruce Pine, NC, Original North Carolina Mineral and Gem Festival—Four days at the beginning of August

Pittsburgh, PA, Carnegie Museum of Natural History Gem and Mineral Show—Last weekend in August

SEPTEMBER

No information available.

OCTOBER

Coloma, CA, Marshall Gold Discovery State Park Gold Rush Days—End of September–beginning of October

Dahlonega, GA, Gold Rush Days—Third weekend in October

Jasper, GA, Pickens County Marble Festival—First weekend in October

Mt. Ida, AR, Quartz Crystal Festival and World Championship Dig—Second weekend in October

Franklin, NC, "Leaf Looker" Gemboree—Second weekend in October

NOVEMBER

Socorro, NM, New Mexico Mineral Symposium—Two days in November

DECEMBER

No information available.

State Gem and Mineral Symbols

STATE	GEMSTONE	MINERAL	STONE/ROCK
Alabama	Star Blue Quartz (1990)	Hematite (1967)	Marble (1969)
Alaska	Jade (1968)	Gold (1968)	
Arizona	Turquoise (1974)		
Arkansas	Diamond	Quartz	Bauxite
California	Benitoite	Gold	Serpentine (1965)
Colorado	Aquamarine (1971)		
Connecticut	Garnet (1977)		
Delaware		Sillimanite	
Florida	Moonstone		Agatized coral
Georgia	Quartz	Staurolite	
Hawaii	Black Coral		
Idaho	Star Garnet (1967)		
Illinois		Fluorite (1965)	
Indiana			Limestone
Iowa			Geode
Kansas			
Kentucky	Freshwater Pearl		
Louisiana	Agate		
Maine		Tourmaline (1971)	
Maryland			
Massachusetts	Rhodonite	Babingtonite	Plymouth Rock, Dighton Rock, Roxbury Conglomerate
Michigan	Isle Royal Greenstone (Chlorostrolite) (1972)		Petosky Stone (1965)
Minnesota	Lake Superior Agate		
Mississippi			Petrified Wood (1976)
Missouri		Galena (1967)	Mozarkite (1967)
Montana			Sapphire & Agate (1969)
Nebraska	Blue Agate (1967)		Prairie Agate (1967)

STATE	GEMSTONE	MINERAL	STONE/ROCK
Nevada	Virgin Valley Blackfire Opal (1987) (Precious) Turquoise (1987) (Semiprecious)	Silver	Sandstone (1987)
New Hampshire	Smoky Quartz	Beryl	Granite
New Jersey			
New Mexico	Turquoise (1967)		
New York	Garnet (1969)		
North Carolina	Emerald (1973)		
North Dakota			
Ohio	Flint (1965)		
Oklahoma			Barite Rose
Oregon	Sunstone (1987)		Thundereggs (1965)
Pennsylvania			
Rhode Island	Bowenite		Cumberlandite
South Carolina	Amethyst		Blue Granite
South Dakota	Fairburn Agate (1966)	Rose Quartz (1966) (Mineral/Stone)	
Tennessee	Tennessee River Pearls		Limestone and Tennessee Marble
Texas	Texas Blue Topaz (1969) Lone Star Cut (1977) (Gemstone Cut)		Petrified Palmwood (1960)
Utah	Topaz		
Vermont			
Virginia			
Washington	Petrified Wood (1975)		
West Virginia			
Wisconsin		Galena (1971)	Red Granite (1971)
Wyoming	Nephrite Jade (1967)		

Finding Your Own Birthstone

Following is a listing of fee dig sites presented in this four-volume guide where you can find your birthstone! Refer to the individual mine listings for more information on individual mines.

Garnet (January Birthstone) Georgia: Dahlonega (SA), Helen (SA); Idaho: St. Maries; Maine: Albany, Bethel, Poland (GS), West Paris (3); Montana: Alder, Helena (S); New Hampshire: Grafton (I); New Mexico: Dixon; New York: North River; North Carolina (*): Almond, Cherokee, Franklin (7), Hiddenite, Little Switzerland (2), Spruce Pine (3) (FT); Nevada: Ely; Washington: Ravensdale (GS)
  Almandine garnets Maine: Poland (GS); Nevada: Ely
  Pyrope garnets North Carolina: Franklin
  Rhodolite garnets North Carolina: Franklin (5)

Amethyst (February Birthstone) Arkansas: Murfreesboro(S); Georgia: Cleveland, Helen (SA); Maine: Bethel (R), West Paris; Montana: Dillon; Nevada: Sun Valley (GS) (crystal scepters); New Hampshire: Grafton (I); New Mexico: Bingham; North Carolina (*): Cherokee, Franklin (5), Little Switzerland, Spruce Pine (3)

Aquamarine or Bloodstone (March Birthstone):
Aquamarine Maine: Bethel, Poland (GS); New Hampshire: Grafton (I); North Carolina (*): Hiddenite, Little Switzerland (5), Marion, Spruce Pine (2) (FT)
  Brushy Creek Aq. North Carolina: Spruce Pine (FT)
  Weisman Aq. North Carolina: Spruce Pine (FT)
Bloodstone No listing

Diamond (April Birthstone) Arkansas: Murfreesboro

Emerald (May Birthstone) Georgia: Cleveland, Dahlonega (SA); North Carolina (*): Cherokee, Franklin, Hiddenite, Little Switzerland (2), Marion, Spruce Pine (2)
Crabtree Emerald North Carolina: Spruce Pine

Moonstone or Pearl (June Birthstone):
Moonstone North Carolina (*): Franklin (7), Little Switzerland, Marion, Spruce Pine
Pearl No listing

Ruby (July Birthstone) Georgia: Cleveland, Dahlonega (SA); Montana: Helena (R); North Carolina (*): Cherokee, Franklin (13), Little Switzerland (2), Spruce Pine (3)

Peridot or Sardonyx (August Birthstone):
Peridot Arkansas: Murfreesboro (S); North Carolina (*): Franklin
Sardonyx No listing

Sapphire (September Birthstone) Georgia: Dahlonega (SA); Montana: Alder (O), Clinton (GS), Gem Mountian, Hamilton, Helena (2), Philipsburg; North Carolina (*): Canton, Cherokee, Franklin (13), Hiddenite, Little Switzerland (2), Spruce Pine

Opal or Tourmaline (October Birthstone):
Opal
  Black opal Nevada: Orovado
  Common opal New Mexico: Deming
  Fire opal Nevada: Gerlach, Orovado
  Hyalite opal Maine: Bethel
  Precious opal Idaho: Spencer; Texas: Alpine
  Wood opal Nevada: Denio
Tourmaline Maine: Poland (GS), West Paris; North Carolina (*): Franklin (7), Hiddenite, Little Switzerland (3), Spruce Pine (3) (FT); Virginia: Amelia
  Black tourmaline Maine: Albany, Bethel, Poland (GS), West Paris; New Hampshire: Grafton (I)
  Gem tourmaline Maine: West Paris
  Green tourmaline Maine: West Paris

Topaz (November Birthstone) Georgia: Cleveland, Helen (SA); Maine: Poland (GS); Montana: Helena (R); New Hampshire: Grafton (I); North Carolina (SA): Cherokee, Franklin (6), Little Switzerland (3), Spruce Pine (3); Texas: Mason (2); Virginia: Amelia
  Blue topaz Colorado: Lake George
  Blue/sherry bicolor Colorado: Lake George
  Phenakitite in topaz crystals Colorado: Lake George (U)
  Pink topaz Washington: Ravensdale (GS)
  Sherry topaz Colorado: Lake George
Turquoise or Lapis Lazuli (December Birthstone):
Turquoise No listing
Lapis Lazuli No listing

The preceding list of birthstones is taken from a list adopted in 1912 by the American National Association of Jewelers ("The Evolution of Birthstones" from *Jewelry & Gems—The Buying Guide* by Antoinette Matlins and A. C. Bonanno; Gemstone Press, 2001).

Finding Your Anniversary Stone

The following is a listing of fee dig sites contained in this four-volume guide where you can find the stone that is associated with a particular anniversary.

First: Gold (Jewelry) Alaska: Fairbanks (3); Arizona: Goldfield; California: Angels Camp (GS), Coloma, Columbia, Jackson, Mariposa, Nevada City, Pine Grove, Placerville; Colorado: Idaho Springs (2); Georgia: Cleveland, Dahlonega (2), Helen; Idaho: Moscow (GS); Indiana: Knightstown; Montana: Alder (O), Helena; North Carolina: Cherokee, Marion, New London, Stanfield, Union Mills; South Dakota: Deadwood, Keystone, Lead

Second: Garnet Georgia: Dahlonega (SA), Helen (SA); Idaho: St. Maries; Maine: Albany, Bethel, Poland (GS), West Paris (3); Montana: Alder, Helena (S); New Hampshire: Grafton (I); New Mexico: Dixon; New York: North River; North Carolina (*): Almond, Cherokee, Franklin (7), Hiddenite, Little Switzerland (2), Spruce Pine (3) (FT); Nevada:Ely; Washington: Ravensdale (GS)
  Almandine garnets Maine: Poland (GS); Nevada: Ely
  Pyrope garnets North Carolina: Franklin
  Rhodolite garnets North Carolina: Franklin (5)

Third: Pearl No listing

Fourth: Blue Topaz Colorado: Lake George

Fifth: Sapphire Georgia: Cleveland, Dahlonega (SA); Montana: Alder (O), Clinton (GS), Gem Mountain, Hamilton, Helena (2), Philipsburg; North Carolina (*): Almond, Canton, Cherokee, Franklin (13), Hiddenite, Little Switzerland (2), Spruce Pine

Sixth: Amethyst Arkansas: Murfreesboro (S); Georgia: Cleveland, Helen (SA); Maine: Bethel (R), West Paris; Montana: Dillon; Nevada: Sun Valley (GS) (crystal scepters); New Hampshire: Grafton (I); New Mexico: Bingham; North Carolina (*): Cherokee, Franklin (5), Little Switzerland, Spruce Pine (3)

Seventh: Onyx No listing

Eighth: Tourmaline Maine: Poland (GS), West Paris; North Carolina (*): Franklin (7), Hiddenite, Little Switzerland (3), Spruce Pine (3) (FT); Virginia: Amelia
  Black tourmaline Maine: Albany, Bethel, Poland (GS), West Paris; New Hampshire: Grafton (I)
  Gem tourmaline Maine: West Paris
  Green tourmaline Maine: West Paris

Ninth: Lapis Lazuli No listing

Tenth: Diamond (Jewelry) Arkansas: Murfreesboro

Eleventh: Turquoise No listing

Twelfth: Jade No listing

Thirteenth: Citrine Georgia: Helen (SA); North Carolina (SA): Almond, Cherokee, Franklin (5), Little Switzerland, Spruce Pine (3)

Fourteenth: Opal
  Black opal Nevada: Orovado
  Common opal New Mexico: Deming
  Fire opal Nevada: Gerlach, Orovado
  Hyalite opal Maine: Bethel
  Precious opal Idaho: Spencer; Texas: Alpine
  Wood opal Nevada: Denio

Fifteenth: Ruby California: Pine Grove; Georgia: Cleveland, Dahlonega (SA); Montana: Helena (R); North Carolina (*): Almond, Cherokee, Franklin (13), Little Switzerland (2), Spruce Pine (3)

Twentieth: Emerald Georgia: Cleveland, Dahlonega (SA); North Carolina (*): Cherokee, Franklin (1), Hiddenite, Little Switzerland (4), Marion, Spruce Pine (2) (also crabtree emerald)

Twenty-fifth: Silver No listing

Thirtieth: Pearl No listing

Thirty-fifth: Emerald Georgia: Cleveland, Dahlonega (SA); North Carolina (*): Cherokee, Franklin, Hiddenite, Little Switzerland (2), Marion, Spruce Pine (2) (also crabree emerald)

Fortieth: Ruby California: Pine Grove; Georgia: Cleveland, Dahlonega (SA); Montana: Helena (R); North Carolina (*): Almond, Cherokee, Franklin (13), Little Switzerland (2), Spruce Pine (3)

Forty-fifth: Sapphire Georgia: Cleveland, Dahlonega (SA); Montana: Alder, Clinton (GS), Gem Mountain, Hamilton, Helena (2), Philipsburg; North Carolina (*): Almond, Canton, Cherokee, Franklin (13), Hiddenite, Little Switzerland (2), Spruce Pine

Fiftieth: Gold Alaska: Fairbanks (3); Arizona: Apache Junction, Goldfield; California: Angels Camp, Coloma, Columbia, Jackson, Mariposa, Nevada City, Pine Grove, Placerville; Colorado: Idaho Springs (2); Georgia: Cleveland, Dahlonega (2), Helen; Idaho: Moscow (GS); Indiana: Knightstown; Montana: Alder (O), Helena; North Carolina: Cherokee, Marion, New London, Stanfield, Union Mills; South Dakota: Deadwood, Keystone, Lead

Fifty-fifth: Alexandrite No listing

Sixtieth: Diamond Arkansas: Murfreesboro

Finding Your Zodiac Stone

The following is a listing of fee dig sites contained in this four-volume guide where you can find the stone that is associated with a particular zodiac sign. Refer to the individual mine listings for more information.

Aquarius (January 21–February 21) Garnet Georgia: Dahlonega (SA), Helen (SA); Idaho: St. Maries; Maine: Albany, Bethel, Poland (GS), West Paris (3); Montana: Alder, Helena (S); New Hampshire: Grafton (I); New Mexico: Dixon; New York: North River; North Carolina (*): Almond, Cherokee, Franklin (7), Hiddenite, Little Switzerland (2), Spruce Pine (3) (FT); Nevada: Ely; Washington: Ravensdale (GS)
  Almandine garnets Maine: Poland (GS); Nevada: Ely
  Pyrope garnets North Carolina: Franklin
  Rhodolite garnets North Carolina: Franklin (5)

Pisces (February 22–March 21) Amethyst Arkansas: Murfreesboro (S); Georgia: Cleveland, Helen (SA); Maine: Albany, Bethel (R), West Paris; Montana: Dillon; Nevada: Sun Valley (GS) (crystal scepters); New Hampshire: Grafton (I); New Mexico: Bingham; New York: North River; North Carolina (*): Almond, Cherokee, Franklin (5), Little Switzerland, Marion, Spruce Pine (3)

Aries (March 21–April 20) Bloodstone (green chalcedony with red spots) No listing

Taurus (April 21–May 21) Sapphire Georgia: Cleveland, Dahlonega (SA); Montana: Alder (O), Clinton (GS), Gem Mountain, Hamilton, Helena (2), Philipsburg; North Carolina (*): Almond, Canton, Cherokee, Franklin (13), Hiddenite, Little Switzerland (2), Spruce Pine

Gemini (May 22–June 21) Agate Arkansas: Murfreesboro(S); Iowa: Bonaporte; Montana: Helena (S); Nevada: Gerlach; New Mexico: Deming (GS); Oklahoma: Kenton (2); Oregon: Yachats; South Dakota: Wall; Texas: Three Rivers; Virginia: Amelia
  Banded agate Texas: Alpine
  Fire agate California: Palo Verde
  Iris agate Texas: Alpine
  Ledge agate Oregon: Madras
  Moss agate Oregon: Madras, Mitchell; Texas: Alpine (2), Wyoming: Shell
  Polka-dot jasp-agate Oregon: Madras
  Plume agate Oregon: Madras
  Pompom agate Texas: Alpine
  Rainbow agate Oregon: Madras
  Red plume agate Texas: Alpine

Cancer (June 22–July 22) Emerald Georgia: Cleveland, Dahlonega (SA); North Carolina (*): Cherokee, Franklin, Hiddenite, Little Switzerland (2), Spruce Pine (2)

Crabtree emerald North Carolina: Spruce Pine

Leo (July 23–August 22) Onyx No listing

Virgo (August 23–September 22) Carnelian No listing

Libra (September 23–October 23) Chrysolite or Peridot:
Peridot Arkansas: Murfreesboro (S); North Carolina (*): Franklin

Scorpio (October 24–November 21) Beryl Maine: Albany, Poland (GS), West Paris; New Mexico: Dixon; North Carolina (*): Little Switzerland (2), Spruce Pine (2); Virginia: Amelia (2)
  Aqua beryl New Hampshire: Grafton (I)
  Blue beryl New Hampshire: Grafton (I)
  Golden beryl North Carolina: Spruce Pine (FT); New Hampshire: Grafton (I)

Sagittarius (November 22–December 21) Topaz Georgia: Cleveland, Helen (SA); Maine: Poland (GS); Montana: Helena (R); New Hampshire: Grafton (I); North Carolina (SA): Cherokee, Franklin (6), Little Switzerland (3), Spruce Pine (3); Texas: Mason (2); Virginia: Amelia
  Blue topaz Colorado: Lake George
  Blue/sherry bicolor Colorado: Lake George
  Phenakitite crystals in topaz Colorado: Lake George (U)
  Pink topaz Washington: Ravensdale (GS)
  Sherry topaz Colorado: Lake George

Capricorn (December 22–January 21) Ruby California: Pine Grove; Georgia: Cleveland, Dahlonega (SA); Montana: Helena (R); North Carolina (*): Almond, Cherokee, Franklin (13), Little Switzerland (2), Spruce Pine (3)

The preceding list of zodiacal stones has been passed on from an early Hindu legend (taken from *Jewelry & Gems—The Buying Guide* by Antoinette Matlins and A. C. Bonanno, Gemstone Press, 2001).

The following is an old Spanish list, probably representing Arab traditions, which ascribes the following stones to various signs of the zodiac (taken from *Jewelry & Gems—The Buying Guide* by Antoinette Matlins and A. C. Bonanno, Gemstone Press, 2001).

Aquarius (January 21–February 21) Amethyst Arkansas: Murfreesboro (S); Georgia: Cleveland, Helen (SA); Maine: Bethel (R), West Paris; Montana: Dillon; New Hampshire: Grafton (I); New Mexico: Bingham; North Carolina (*): Almond, Cherokee, Franklin (5), Little Switzerland, Marion, Spruce Pine (3)
Crystal scepters Nevada: Sun Valley (GS)
Pisces (February 22–March 21) Undistinguishable

Aries (March 21–April 20) Quartz Arkansas: Hot Springs, Jessieville, Mt. Ida (7) (Y), Murfreesboro (S), Paron; California: Pine Grove; Colorado: Lake George; Maine: Poland (GS); Montana: Dillon, Helena; New Hampshire: Grafton; New Mexico: Bingham, Deming, Dixon, Socorro (Y); Texas: Alpine; Virginia: Amelia; Washington: Ravensdale (GS)

Blue Georgia: Lincolnton; North Carolina: Marion

Clear North Carolina (*): Franklin, Hiddenite, Little Switzerland, Marion, Spruce Pine

Milky Maine: Bethel

Orange Maine: West Paris

Parallel growth Maine: West Paris

Pseudocubic crystals Maine: West Paris

Rose Georgia: Helen (SA); Maine: Albany, West Paris; New Hampshire: Grafton (I); North Carolina (*): Franklin, Little Switzerland, Marion

Rose (gem quality) Maine: Albany, West Paris

Rutilated North Carolina (*): Little Switzerland, Spruce Pine

Smoky Georgia: Helen (SA); Maine: Bethel, West Paris; New Hampshire: Grafton (I); North Carolina (*): Almond, Cherokee, Franklin (6), Hiddenite, Little Switzerland (2), Marion, Spruce Pine (2)

Smoky (gem quality) Maine: West Paris

Quartz "diamonds"

Lake Co. "diamonds" (moon tears) California: Lake County

Cape May "diamonds" New Jersey: Cape May

Herkimer "diamonds" New York: Herkimer, Little Falls, Middleville, St. Johnsville

Taurus (April 21–May 21) Rubies, Diamonds:

Rubies California: Pine Grove; Georgia: Dahlonega (SA); Montana: Helena (R); North Carolina (*): Almond, Cherokee, Franklin (13), Little Switzerland (2), Spruce Pine (3)

Diamonds Arkansas: Murfreesboro

Gemini (May 22–June 21) Sapphire Georgia: Cleveland, Dahlonega (SA); Montana: Alder (O), Clinton (GS), Gem Mountain, Hamilton, Helena (2), Philipsburg; North Carolina (*): Almond, Canton, Cherokee, Franklin (13), Hiddenite, Little Switzerland (2), Spruce Pine

Cancer (June 22–July 22) Agate and Beryl:

Agate Arkansas: Murfreesboro (S); Iowa: Bonaporte; Montana: Helena (S); Nevada: Gerlach; New Mexico: Deming (GS); Oklahoma: Kenton (2); Oregon: Yachats; South Dakota: Wall; Texas: Three Rivers; Virginia: Amelia

Banded agate Texas: Alpine

Fire agate California: Palo Verde

Iris agate Texas: Alpine

Ledge agate Oregon: Madras

Moss agate Oregon: Madras, Mitchell; Texas: Alpine (2), Wyoming: Shell

Polka-dot agate Oregon: Madras (R)

Plume agate Oregon: Madras
Pompom agate Texas: Alpine
Rainbow agate Oregon: Madras (R)
Red plume agate Texas: Alpine
Beryl Maine: Albany, Poland (GS), West Paris; New Mexico, Dixon; North Carolina (*): Little Switzerland (2), Spruce Pine (2); Virginia: Amelia (2)
   Aqua beryl New Hampshire: Grafton (I)
   Blue beryl New Hampshire: Grafton (I)
   Golden beryl North Carolina: Spruce Pine (FT); New Hampshire: Grafton (I)

Leo (July 23–August 22) Topaz Georgia: Cleveland, Helen (SA); Maine: Poland (GS); Montana: Helena (R); New Hampshire: Grafton (I); North Carolina (SA): Cherokee, Franklin (6), Little Switzerland (3), Spruce Pine (3); Texas: Mason (2); Virginia: Amelia
   Blue topaz Colorado: Lake George
   Blue/sherry bicolor Colorado: Lake George
   Phenakitite crystals in topaz Colorado: Lake George (U)
   Pink topaz Washington: Ravensdale (GS)
   Sherry topaz Colorado: Lake George

Virgo (August 23–September 22) Bloodstone (green chalcedony with red spots)
   No listing

Libra (September 23–October 23) Jasper Arkansas: Murfreesboro (S); California: Pine Grove; Montana: Helena; Oklahoma: Kenton; Oregon: Madras, Yachats; Texas: Alpine
   Brown jasper New Mexico: Deming
   Chocolate jasper New Mexico: Deming
   Orange jasper New Mexico: Deming
   Picture jasper Oregon: Mitchell
   Pink jasper New Mexico: Deming
   Variegated jasper New Mexico: Deming
   Yellow jasper New Mexico: Deming

Scorpio (October 24–November 21) Garnet Georgia: Dahlonega (SA), Helen (SA); Idaho: St. Maries; Maine: Albany, Bethel, Poland (GS), West Paris (3); Montana: Alder, Helena (S); New Hampshire: Grafton (I); New Mexico: Dixon; North Carolina (*): Almond, Cherokee, Franklin (7), Hiddenite, Little Switzerland (2), Spruce Pine (3) (FT); Nevada: Ely; Washington: Ravensdale (GS)
   Almandine garnets Maine: Poland (GS); Nevada: Ely
   Pyrope garnets North Carolina: Franklin
   Rhodolite garnets North Carolina: Franklin (5)

Sagittarius (November 22–December 21) Emerald Georgia: Cleveland, Dahlonega (SA); North Carolina (*): Cherokee, Franklin, Hiddenite, Little Switzerland (2), Marion, Spruce Pine (2)
Crabtree emerald North Carolina: Spruce Pine

Capricorn (December 22–January 21) Chalcedony New Mexico: Deming
Blue chalcedony Nevada: Sun Valley (GS)

Some Publications on Gems and Minerals

Lapidary Journal

Subscriptions
P.O. Box 56553
Boulder, CO 80322
(800) 676-4336
www.lapidaryjournal.com

Rocks & Minerals

5341 Thrasher Dr.
Cincinnati, OH 45247
Phone: (800) 365-9753
Fax: (202) 293-6130
www.mineralart.com/rocks_and_
minerals

Rock & Gem

c/o Miller Magazines, Inc.
4880 Market Street
Ventura, CA 93003-7783
Phone: (805) 644-3824
www.rockngem.com

Gold Prospector

Gold Prospectors Association of America, Inc.
P.O. Box 891509
Temecula, CA 92589
Phone: (909) 699-4749
www.goldprospectors.org

Send Us Your Feedback

Disclaimer

The authors have made every reasonable effort to obtain accurate information for this guide. However, much of the information in the book is based on material provided by the sites and has not been verified independently. The information given here does not represent recommendations, but merely a listing of information. The authors and publisher accept no liability for any accident or loss incurred when readers are patronizing the establishments listed herein. The authors and publisher accept no liability for errors or omissions. Since sites may shut down or change their hours of operations or fees without advance notice, please call the site before your visit for confirmation before planning your trip.

The authors would appreciate being informed of changes, additions, or deletions that should be made to this guide. To that end, a form is attached, which can be filled out and mailed to the authors for use in future editions of the guide.

Have We Missed Your Mine or Museum?

This is a project with a national scope, based on extensive literature search, phone and mail inquiry, and personal investigation. However, we are dealing with a business in which many owners are retiring or closing and selling their sites. In addition, many of the mines, guide services, and smaller museums have limited publicity, known more by word of mouth than by publication. Thus, it is possible that your operation or one you have visited was not included in this guide. Please let us know if you own or operate a mine, guide service, or museum, or have visited a mine, guide service, or museum that is not in the guide. It will be considered for inclusion in the next edition of the guide. Send updates to:

Treasure Hunter's Guides
GemStone Press
Route 4, Sunset Farm Offices
P.O. Box 237
Woodstock, VT 05091

Do You Have a Rockhounding Story to Share?

If you have a special story about a favorite dig site, send it in for consideration for use in the next edition of the guide.

A Request to Mines and Museums:

For sites already included in this guide, we request that you put us on your annual mailing list so that we may have an updated copy of your information.

Notes on Museums

In this guide we have included listings of museums with noteworthy gem, mineral, or rock collections. We particularly tried to find local museums displaying gems or minerals native to the area where they are located. This list is by no means complete, and if you feel we missed an important listing, let us know by completing the following form. Since these guides focus specifically on gems and minerals, only those exhibits have been recognized in the museum listings, and we do not mention any collection or exhibits of fossils. See our sequel on fossils for information on fossil collections.

READER'S CONTRIBUTION

I would like to supply the following information for possible inclusion in the next edition of *The Treasure Hunter's Guide*:

Type of entry: ☐ fee dig ☐ guide service ☐ museum ☐ mine tour
☐ annual event

This is a: ☐ new entry ☐ entry currently in the guide

Nature of info: ☐ addition ☐ change ☐ deletion

Please describe (brochure and additional info may be attached):

_____

_____

_____

_____

Please supply the following in case we need to contact you regarding your information:

Name: _____

Address: _____

_____

_____

Phone: ( ) _____

E-mail: _____

Date: _____

FIELD NOTES

FIELD NOTES

FIELD NOTES

FIELD NOTES

FIELD NOTES

FIELD NOTES

FIELD NOTES

FIELD NOTES

FIELD NOTES

FIELD NOTES

FIELD NOTES

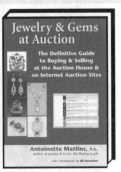

CAMEOS OLD & NEW, 3RD EDITION
by Anna M. Miller, G.G.

Newly updated and expanded, *Cameos Old & New,* 3rd Ed., is a **concise, easy-to-understand guide** enabling anyone—from beginner to antique dealer—to recognize and evaluate quality and value in cameos, and avoid the pitfalls of purchasing mediocre pieces, fakes and forgeries.

6" x 9", 312 pp., over 300 photographs and illustrations, 130 in full color; index
Quality Paperback, ISBN 0-943763-36-3 **$19.95**

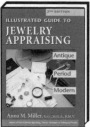

ILLUSTRATED GUIDE TO JEWELRY APPRAISING,
2ND EDITION • *Antique, Period, Modern*
by Anna M. Miller, G.G., R.M.V.

This beautifully illustrated guide **provides step-by-step instruction** in jewelry identification and dating, reviews the responsibilities of the appraiser, and describes in detail virtually every style of antique and period jewelry for the hobbyist and serious collector alike.

8½" x 11", 216 pp., over 150 photographs and illustrations; index
Hardcover, ISBN 0-943763-23-1 **$39.95**

GEMS & JEWELRY APPRAISING, 2ND EDITION
Techniques of Professional Practice
by Anna M. Miller, G.G., R.M.V.

The **premier guide to the standards, procedures and ethics of appraising gems, jewelry and other valuables.** *Gems & Jewelry Appraising* offers all the information that jewelers, gemologists and students will need to establish an appraisal business, handle various kinds of appraisals and provide an accurate, verifiable estimate of value.

8½" x 11", 256 pp., over 130 photographs and illustrations; index
Hardcover, ISBN 0-943763-10-X **$39.95**

TREASURE HUNTER'S GEM & MINERAL GUIDES TO THE U.S.A.
2ND EDITIONS
Where & How to Dig, Pan and Mine Your Own Gems & Minerals
—IN 4 REGIONAL VOLUMES—
by Kathy J. Rygle *and* Stephen F. Pedersen • *Preface by* Antoinette Matlins, P.G., *author of* Gem Identification Made Easy

From rubies, opals and gold, to emeralds, aquamarine and diamonds, each guide offers **state-by-state details on more than 250 gems and minerals** and the affordable "fee dig" sites where they can be found. Each guide covers:

- **Equipment & Clothing:** What you need and where to find it.
- **Mining Techniques:** Step-by-step instructions.
- **Gem and Mineral Sites:** Directions & maps, hours, fees, and more.
- **Museums and Mine Tours**

All guides: 6" x 9", Quality Paperback Original, Illustrations, maps & photos, indexes. **$14.95 each**
Northeast (CT, DC, DE, IL, IN, MA, MD, ME, MI, NH, NJ, NY, OH, PA, RI, VT, WI)
208 pp., ISBN 0-943763-39-8
Northwest (AK, IA, ID, MN, MT, ND, NE, OR, SD, WA, WY)
176 pp., ISBN 0-943763-37-1
Southeast (AL, AR, FL, GA, KY, LA, MO, MS, NC, SC, TN, VA, WV)
192 pp., ISBN 0-943763-40-1
Southwest (AZ, CA, CO, HI, KS, NM, NV, OK, TX, UT)
208 pp., ISBN 0-943763-38-X

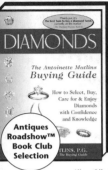

DIAMONDS: THE ANTOINETTE MATLINS BUYING GUIDE
How to Select, Buy, Care for & Enjoy Diamonds with Confidence and Knowledge
by Antoinette Matlins, P.G.

Practical, comprehensive, and easy to understand, this book includes price guides for old and new cuts and for fancy-color, treated, and synthetic diamonds. **Explains in detail** how to read diamond grading reports and offers important advice for after buying a diamond. **The "unofficial bible" for all diamond buyers who want to get the most for their money.**

6" x 9", 220 pp., 12 full-color pages & many b/w illustrations and photos; index
Quality Paperback Original, ISBN 0-943763-32-0 **$16.95**

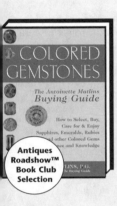

COLORED GEMSTONES:
THE ANTOINETTE MATLINS BUYING GUIDE
How to Select, Buy, Care for & Enjoy Sapphires, Emeralds, Rubies and Other Colored Gems with Confidence and Knowledge
by Antoinette Matlins, P.G.

This practical, comprehensive, easy-to-understand guide **provides in depth** all the information you need to buy colored gems with confidence. Includes price guides for popular gems, opals, and synthetic stones. Provides examples of gemstone grading reports and offers important advice for after buying a gemstone. **Shows anyone shopping for colored gemstones how to get the most for their money.**

6" x 9", 224 pp., 16 full-color pages & many b/w illustrations and photos; index
Quality Paperback Original, ISBN 0-943763-33-9 **$16.95**

THE PEARL BOOK, 3RD EDITION:
THE DEFINITIVE BUYING GUIDE
How to Select, Buy, Care for & Enjoy Pearls
by Antoinette Matlins, P.G.
COMPREHENSIVE • EASY TO READ • PRACTICAL

This comprehensive, authoritative guide tells readers everything they need to know about pearls to fully understand and appreciate them, and avoid any unexpected—and costly—disappointments, now and in future generations.

- A journey into the rich history and romance surrounding pearls.
- The five factors that determine pearl value & judging pearl quality.
- What to look for, what to look out for: How to spot fakes. Treatments.
- Differences between natural, cultured and imitation pearls, and ways to separate them.
- Comparisons of all types of pearls, in every size and color, from every pearl-producing country.

6" x 9", 232 pp., 16 full-color pages & over 250 color and b/w illustrations and photos; index
Quality Paperback, ISBN 0-943763-35-5 **$19.95**

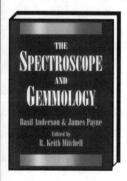

Buy Your *"Tools of the Trade"*...

Gem Identification Instruments directly from *GemStone Press*

Whatever instrument you need, GemStone Press can help.
Use our convenient order form, or contact us directly for assistance.

Complete Pocket Instrument Set
SPECIAL SAVINGS!
BUY THIS ESSENTIAL TRIO AND SAVE 12%
Used together, you can identify 85% of all gems with these three
portable, pocket-sized instruments—the essential trio.
10X Triplet Loupe • Chelsea Filter • Calcite Dichroscope

Pocket Instrument Set:
Standard: With Standard 10X Loupe • OPL Dichroscope • Chelsea Filter **only $144.95**
Deluxe: With Bausch & Lomb 10X Loupe • EZVIEW Dichroscope • Chelsea Filter **only $179.95**

ITEM / QUANTITY	PRICE EA.*	TOTAL $
Pocket Instrument Sets		
_____ **Standard:** With Standard 10X Loupe • OPL Dichroscope • Chelsea Filter	$144.95	$ _____
_____ **Deluxe:** With Bausch & Lomb 10X Loupe • EZVIEW Dichroscope • Chelsea Filter	$179.95	_____
Loupes—Professional Jeweler's 10X Triplet Loupes		
_____ Bausch & Lomb 10X Triplet Loupe	$44.00	_____
_____ Standard 10X Triplet Loupe	$29.00	_____
_____ Darkfield Diamond View	$58.95	_____
• Spot filled diamonds, other enhancements and zoning instantly. Operates with large maglite (optional).		
_____ RosGem Loupe-Fillfinder	$69.95	
Analyzer		
_____ Gem Analyzer	$285.00	_____
• Combines Darkfield Loupe, Polariscope, and Immersion Cell		
Calcite Dichroscopes		
_____ Dichroscope (EZVIEW)	$115.00	_____
_____ Dichroscope (OPL)	$89.95	_____
Color Filters		
_____ Chelsea Filter	$44.95	_____
_____ Synthetic Emerald Filter Set (Hanneman)	$32.00	_____
_____ Tanzanite Filter (Hanneman)	$28.00	_____
_____ Bead Buyer's & Parcel Picker's Filter Set (Hanneman)	$24.00	_____
Diamond Testers and Tweezers		
_____ SSEF Diamond-Type Spotter	$150.00	_____
_____ Diamondnite Dual Tester	$269.00	_____
_____ Diamond Tweezers/Locking	$10.65	_____
_____ Diamond Tweezers/Non-Locking	$7.80	_____
Jewelry Cleaners		
_____ Ionic Cleaner—Home size model	$69.95	_____
_____ Ionic Solution—16 oz. bottle	$20.00	_____

See Over for More Instruments

Buy Your *"Tools of the Trade..."*

Gem Identification Instruments directly from *GemStone Press*

Whatever instrument you need, GemStone Press can help.
Use our convenient order form, or contact us directly for assistance.

ITEM / QUANTITY	PRICE EA.*	TOTAL $
Lamps—Ultraviolet & High Intensity		
_____ Small LW/SW (UVP)	$71.00	_____
_____ Large LW/SW (UVP)	$189.00	_____
_____ Viewing Cabinet for Large Lamp (UVP)	$147.00	_____
_____ **Purchase Large Lamp & Cabinet together**	$299.00	_____
for $299 and save $37.00		
_____ Dialite Flip Lamp (Eickhorst)	$64.95	_____
For Use with the SSEF Diamond-Type Spotter		
_____ SSEF High-Intensity Shortwave Lamp	$499.00	_____
_____ Portable SSEF High-Intensity Shortwave Lamp	$300.00	_____
Other Light Sources		
_____ Large Maglite	$15.00	_____
_____ Flex Light	$29.95	_____
Refractometers		
_____ Standard Refractometer (Eickhorst)	$625.00	_____
_____ Pocket Refractometer (Eickhorst)	$495.00	_____
_____ Refractive Index Liquid 1.81—10 gram	$42.50	_____
Spectroscopes		
_____ Spectroscope—Pocket-sized model (OPL)	$89.00	_____
_____ Spectroscope—Desk model w/stand (OPL)	$225.00	_____

Shipping/Insurance per order in the U.S.: $4.95 first item,   SHIPPING/INS. $_____
$3.00 each add'l item; $7.95 total for pocket instrument set.

Outside the U.S.: Please specify *insured* shipping method you prefer
and provide a credit card number for payment.   **TOTAL $ _____****

Check enclosed for $ _____ (Payable to: GEMSTONE PRESS)

Charge my credit card: ❑ Visa ❑ MasterCard

Name on Card _____

Cardholder Address: Street _____

City/State/Zip _____

Credit Card # _____ Exp. Date _____

Signature _____ Phone (_____)_____

Please send to: ❑ Same as Above ❑ Address Below

Name _____

Street _____

City/State/Zip _____ Phone (_____)_____

Phone, mail, fax, or e-mail orders to:

GEMSTONE PRESS, P.O. Box 237, Woodstock, VT 05091

Tel: (802) 457-4000 • Fax: (802) 457-4004 • Credit Card Orders: (800) 962-4544

sales@gemstonepress.com • www.gemstonepress.com

Generous Discounts on Quantity Orders

TOTAL SATISFACTION GUARANTEE
If for any reason you're not completely delighted
with your purchase, return it in resellable condition
within 30 days for a full refund.

See Over for More Instruments

*Prices, manufacturing specifications, and terms subject to change
without notice. Orders accepted subject to availability.

**All orders must be prepaid by credit card, money order or check
in U.S. funds drawn on a U.S. bank.

Please send me:

CAMEOS OLD & NEW, 3RD EDITION
_____ copies at $19.95 (Quality Paperback) *plus s/h**

COLORED GEMSTONES: THE ANTOINETTE MATLINS BUYING GUIDE
_____ copies at $16.95 (Quality Paperback) *plus s/h**

DIAMONDS: THE ANTOINETTE MATLINS BUYING GUIDE
_____ copies at $16.95 (Quality Paperback) *plus s/h**

ENGAGEMENT & WEDDING RINGS: THE DEFINITIVE BUYING GUIDE, 3RD EDITION
_____ copies at $18.95 (Quality Paperback) *plus s/h**

GEM IDENTIFICATION MADE EASY, 2ND EDITION:
A HANDS-ON GUIDE TO MORE CONFIDENT BUYING & SELLING
_____ copies at $34.95 (Hardcover) *plus s/h**

GEMS & JEWELRY APPRAISING, 2ND EDITION
_____ copies at $39.95 (Hardcover) *plus s/h**

ILLUSTRATED GUIDE TO JEWELRY APPRAISING, 2ND EDITION
_____ copies at $39.95 (Hardcover) *plus s/h**

JEWELRY & GEMS AT AUCTION: THE DEFINITIVE GUIDE TO BUYING & SELLING
AT THE AUCTION HOUSE & ON INTERNET AUCTION SITES
_____ copies at $19.95 (Quality Paperback) *plus s/h**

JEWELRY & GEMS: THE BUYING GUIDE, 5TH EDITION
_____ copies at $18.95 (Quality Paperback) *plus s/h**
_____ copies at $24.95 (Hardcover) *plus s/h**

THE PEARL BOOK, 3RD EDITION: THE DEFINITIVE BUYING GUIDE
_____ copies at $19.95 (Quality Paperback) *plus s/h**

THE SPECTROSCOPE AND GEMMOLOGY
_____ copies at $69.95 (Hardcover) *plus s/h**

TREASURE HUNTER'S GEM & MINERAL GUIDES TO THE U.S.A., 2ND EDITIONS:
WHERE & HOW TO DIG, PAN AND MINE YOUR OWN GEMS & MINERALS—
IN 4 REGIONAL VOLUMES $14.95 per copy (Quality Paperback) *plus s/h**
_____ copies of NE States _____ copies of SE States _____ copies of NW States _____ copies of SW States

* In U.S.: Shipping/Handling: $3.75 for 1st book, $2.00 each additional book.
   Outside U.S.: Specify shipping method (insured) and provide a credit card number for payment.

Check enclosed for $_____ (Payable to: GEMSTONE Press)
Charge my credit card: ❑ Visa ❑ MasterCard
Name on Card (PRINT) _____
Cardholder Address: Street _____
City/State/Zip _____ E-mail _____
Credit Card # _____ Exp. Date _____
Signature _____ Phone (____)_____
Please send to: ❑ Same as Above ❑ Address Below
Name (PRINT) _____
Street _____
City/State/Zip _____ Phone (____)_____

Phone, mail, fax, or e-mail orders to:

GEMSTONE PRESS, Sunset Farm Offices,
Rte. 4, P.O. Box 237, Woodstock, VT 05091
Tel: (802) 457-4000 • *Fax:* (802) 457-4004
Credit Card Orders: (800) 962-4544
sales@gemstonepress.com
www.gemstonepress.com

Generous Discounts on Quantity Orders

Prices subject
to change

Try Your Bookstore First